a message to MILLENNIALS

a message to MILLENNIALS

what your parents didn't tell you and your employer needs you to know

CHARLIE "T" JONES
and TRACEY C. JONES

A MESSAGE TO MILLENNIALS:
What Your Parents Didn't Tell You
and Your Employer Needs You to Know

Published by Tremendous Leadership
PO Box 267
Boiling Springs, PA 17007
717-701-8159
www.Tremendousleadership.com

ISBN: 978-1-936354-52-8

Cover Design: Karen Webb

First Edition

Printed in the United States of America.

OTHER BOOKS

By: Charlie "Tremendous" Jones

Life is Tremendous

Kids are Tremendous

Humor is Tremendous:
A Comical Collection of Quips and Quotes, Jests and Jokes

Books are Tremendous:
Life-Changing Classics, Vol. VIII

Being Tremendous:
The Life, Lessons, and Legacy of Charlie "Tremendous" Jones

The Key to Excellence:
Life-Changing Classics, Vol. XIII

Forgiveness is Tremendous:
Experience the Secret that Will Change Your Life

It's All About Jesus:
Three Best-selling Authors, One Dynamic Savior

The Mystery of Self-motivation:
Life-Changing Classics, Vol. XVI

The Price of Leadership:
Life-Changing Classics, Vol. XI

The Three Decisions:
Life-Changing Classics, Vol. XV

Eternal Life Insurance Policies

Quotes are Tremendous

OTHER BOOKS

By: Tracey C. Jones

Beyond Tremendous:
Raising the Bar on Life

Saucy Aussie Living:
Top 10 Tricks for Getting a Second Leash on Life

True Blue Leadership:
Top 10 Tricks From the Chief Motivational Hound

Boxcar Indy:
A Square Dog in a Round World

Boxcar Indy Goes to Doggy World

From Underdog to Wonder Dog:
Top 10 Ways to Lead Your Pack

No, No, Roscoe!

TABLE OF CONTENTS

DEDICATION

This book is dedicated to my father, the late and great, Charlie "Tremendous" Jones. I never met anyone who was such a perfect blend of power and humility. I watched him hustle and build his business until his last breath. I also saw him stop everything so he could be of encouragement to anyone at anytime. He taught me to see the beauty and grace in not only being a leader, but in being a follower. I am honored to carry on what he started and thankful to all of you who are engaged in his legacy.

PREFACE

By: Tracey C. Jones

Although this book calls out millennials in the title, its message is as old as time. I interact with many tremendous millennials. The ones who come to my presentations are intent on learning how to become the leaders they've always dreamed of being. I have written this book especially for you. I was raised by the Greatest Generation. I am half Baby Boomer/half Gen X. So I walk in both worlds. Although I could be your mother, think of me more as the cool older sister whom you desperately want to be like when you grow up (please!).

Those of us brought up by the Greatest Generation were raised by the velvet fist. We were disciplined frequently, sometimes with love and sometimes without. But we knew without question where the boundaries were. We knew there were consequences when we messed up, and we knew that crying was for babies (unless someone or something died). They assumed we were strong, not fragile.

The only opinions we worried about were those of our parents, certainly not the World Wide Web of judgment with which you have been raised. Trust me when I say my heart breaks for you. If someone said something nasty to us, our feelings got hurt but not our self-esteem. Sticks and stones broke our bones, but we learned to suck it up. When we entered the cold, cruel world, we were ready because we were tough.

We didn't fear change. We feared failing to launch.

We played games with actual children in the actual great outdoors, games like "Follow the Leader" and "Simon Says." We sat in church quietly without gadgets because children were to be seen and not heard. We were raised on a principle from the book of Proverbs, "Spare the rod, spoil the child." Even during my plebe years at the military academy, we were only allowed five responses to any question under the sun. Can you imagine if you were only allowed the following five responses during your staff meetings? "Yes, sir/ma'am. No, sir/ma'am. Sir/ma'am, I do not know but will find out. No excuse, sir/ma'am. Roger Wilco, sir/ma'am."

But it was drilled into us at an early age that until we had something worthwhile to say, until we had actually done something of value, until we could contribute to the solutions and not just post selfies, no one would care one iota about us. And you know what? It didn't hurt our feelings at all. In fact, it made perfect sense.

I first read *A Message to Garcia* in 2010. I'd heard it referenced many times throughout my military and corporate careers. When I finally read it, it took all of ten minutes. Such power! No wonder it has more than forty million copies in print, making it one of the most widely read books.

Do you know what its message is? *Just do it*. When someone gives you a task, don't pass the buck, don't look at them sideways, don't whine, don't complain, just get to work figuring it out, and get it done!

I can remember watching the movie *Patton* with my father when I was a teenager. During the part when General Patton was dressing down the wounded soldier, I exclaimed, "Man, is that guy mean!" To which my father replied, "Just wait until you have to work with people." I had no idea what he meant at the time, but many years later, I sure do. People are lazy, they often don't take ownership, and they need to be directed, but they will, nevertheless, snap at you for not allowing them autonomy. It's just the way we are. It's part of the human condition.

But every now and then, something comes across our paths that enlightens us and reveals that we are both the problem AND the solution to our problem. In my case, it was the guidance of my father, my teachers, my commanders, my bosses, friends, and even adversaries, plus the countless books I've read, that made me unlearn what I thought I knew so I could relearn it in a new way.

Most importantly, what all of this taught me, was that in order to be a tremendous *leader*, I had to first master how to be a tremendous *follower*. You will never amount to anything unless you are able to put your ego and feelings aside for the greater good. That's something my generation learned in spades, and it's something I hope to pass on to the next generation.

You want to be somebody. I get it. All of us who've gone before you felt exactly the same way. You want the same things we wanted—to be valued, to have a place to go, *to matter*. Please, trust me. The sooner you learn how to be an effective, enthusiastic member of your team—the sooner you will understand the functions of followership and the sooner you will grow into the tremendous leader you hope to become.

So let me share with you some of the things I've learned so you can develop into the leaders we so desperately need.

INTRODUCTION

No one is born a leader. Every great leader learned at the feet of another. Even those born to nobility had to learn their skills. History is littered with the names of monarchs who led their countries to ruin because they never learned to lead.

The surest road to leadership is *followership.* Leadership and followership are two sides of the same coin. The leader and follower are complementary. You can't have one without the other. Much has been written about leadership, from the Great Man theory to Servant Leadership, but very little has been written about followership. More and more young people are desperately trying to discover the secret of becoming a leader when the most obvious answer is to first become an exemplary follower. Technology has given many of us a

Leadership and followership are two sides of the same coin.

false sense of experience and knowledge. It has exposed us to numerous different things, but it hasn't transformed us. Only hard work and the persistence to be a dedicated follower can do that.

Show me the type of follower you are today, and I'll show you the type of leader you'll be tomorrow. Followership is the cornerstone of leadership. Comedian Phil Silvers said it best: "If you wanna be top banana, you gotta start at the bottom of the bunch." Even Aristotle decried wanting to start at the top instead of working your way up. You cannot skip this step. You cannot get rich quick, and you cannot become a leader quick. Only time, effort, and results will get you there.

> **Technology has given many of us a false sense of experience and knowledge.**

Fifty years ago my father and co-author, Charlie "Tremendous" Jones, wrote *Life is Tremendous,* in which he outlined The Seven Laws of Leadership. We've updated and rereleased these laws here and included something brand new: The Seven Functions of Followership. If you never learned tremendous followership tips when you were young, do not fear. It's never too late, and in the book, we'll outline the seven functions of leadership and followership that will put you on the path towards greater things in your personal and professional lives.

As followers, understanding our role on the team is critical. We are not just cogs in the wheel of a money-making machine. Without us, the system would grind to a halt. Effective followers are critical components of every organization's success. No man is an island unto himself, and as Warren Bennis so famously said, "None of us is as smart as all of us."

As a follower, you can serve alongside the leader and, in essence, become the *lead follower.* The surest path to the leadership chair is through serving at the side of the leader. The lead follower honors the leader and makes him or her look good. Do this and you will begin the internal transformation to becoming a leader without even realizing it.

> **You'll no longer have to ask when you'll become a leader. You'll recognize that you already are one.**

One last point: We vacillate between the roles of leader and follower numerous times a day. One is not "better" or more important than the other. Leader-follower distinctions should be invisible. So the more proficient you become in each of these roles, the better able you'll be to not only go with the flow but to bloom wherever you are planted. Life's a journey full of unexpected destinations. When you keep your mind and heart open to fulfilling whatever role is needed at any particular time, your life will become enriched. You'll no longer have to ask when you'll become a leader. You'll recognize that you already are one. May the Seven Functions of Followership help you discover how you can be of the greatest use to your business, church, family, or group.

MILLENNIAL MOMENT #1:

Have you ever said this?

This place sucks!

So what are you going to do about it? Take responsibility for your surroundings! Look, a job description is nothing more than words on a paper. A cubicle is nothing more than an inanimate coalition of partitions. You need to get that "work" is NOT a four-letter word. It CAN be a tremendous experience. Every. Single. Day. They only call it "work" because "Disneyland" was already taken.

You can fight, but you won't win. In fact, you may ruin any chance of upward mobility anywhere else. You can take flight, but you'll quickly realize it's the same thing in a different surrounding. Or you can find a way to adapt. But that means taking responsibility for fixing this problem. That means you have to get your head in the game.

From the time you wake up, through your commute, including your quick stop at Starbucks or Mickey D's, to the parking deck, the elevator, the long hall of cubbies that make up your office gopher farm, all the way to the corner office where the world's biggest jerk has been pacing for 45 minutes waiting for you to trip his motion sensors, the universe itself on some days seems hell-bent on ruining your day before it even starts. It's the traffic. It's the weather. The Web is down. Email is slow. Suzy from two cubbies over won't shut up.

It's always something. There will always be something. The person responsible for your happiness is... you.

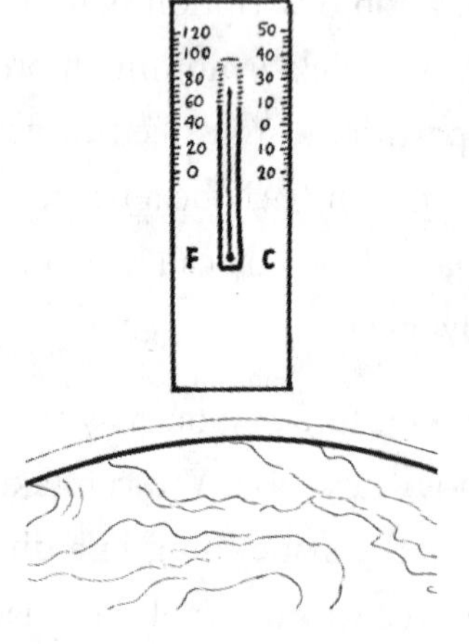

Don't simply reflect the temperature of your work environment: Set it. Create the cultural comfort level where you function best.

THE FIRST LAW OF LEADERSHIP:

Get Excited About Your Work

By: Charlie "Tremendous" Jones

Once in a while you hear it said, "Show me someone who will work, and I will show you a success." And I say, "Show me someone who says that, and I will show you an idiot." Work in itself will not do it. I know; I almost worked myself out of existence a dozen times.

Why do some people work and work and work and never have anything to show for it while others don't seem to work at all yet they have great results? The First Law of Leadership is not *work* as we usually think of it — though it still takes work — but *getting excited about your work.*

I know what you're thinking. "Jones, don't you know it's easy to get excited about something glamorous like what you do or what an executive does? If you had this lousy job of mine, you wouldn't talk like that." I'll let you in on a secret. *Work*, wherever you find it, implies detail, monotony, preparation, striving, and weariness. That's what we all have to overcome, no matter what our work is.

Sure, it's easy to get excited about something I'm not doing. But if *I* have to do it, and I have to learn and grow and plan and persevere — then work isn't much fun. But the First Law of Leadership is getting excited about *my* work, not about someone else's, and not about the work I'm going to do *someday.* The First Law of Leadership tells me to get excited about the miserable job I have right now. And, you know, if I can get excited about it while it's miserable, it's going to be tremendous if it ever gets pleasant!

A young man came into my office after graduating number two in his class at an Ivy League school. He said, "Mr. Jones, I've heard about you. I've been interviewed by this company and that company and none of them appealed to me. I thought you could help me find what I would like to do."

Oh, one of those poor fellows, I thought. *I'll give him a little shock treatment.* I replied, "You'd like me to help *you* find what you'd like to do? How can I help you find what you'd like to do when I haven't been able to find what *I* would like to do?"

He said, "Don't you like what you're doing?" I bellowed, "I *hate* it! They don't pay very much money to do the things I like to do!"

Do you know what I like? I like to relax; I like to *talk* about work. I like vacations, conventions, commissions, salary increases, long luncheons. What do I get? Headaches, heartbreaks, turndowns! But you know what I've been learning? If I don't get excited about what I *don't* like to do, I won't get much that I *can* get excited about.

Life is not about doing what you like to do. Life is about doing what you *ought* to do. People who do what they like to do eventually discover that what they thought they liked to do, they don't like to do. But people who learn to do what they don't like to do but what they *ought* to do, eventually discover that the thing they didn't like to do becomes the thing they do like to do.

> **Life is not about doing what you like to do. Life is about doing what you *ought* to do.**

When I was 25, they paid me $75,000 a year to do things I didn't like to do. When I was 30 they paid me $175,000 a year to do things I didn't like to do. When I was 35, they paid me $375,000 a year to do things I didn't like to do. The salary didn't make those jobs worthwhile, but my efforts and the results were important. Life isn't a matter of doing what you like to do. It's a matter of doing what you ought to do and need to do.

During the Great Depression everyone learned that the most exciting thing in the world was to be able to work. To have a job, any kind of a job, was a privilege.

Today everyone's looking for the right kind of job. Someone says, "I'm trying to find a job that fits me." I say, "I hope you get something better than that." Remember: God never made the job that could make a person, but anyone who can get excited about work can make a job.

Why is enthusiasm for work so important to success? Let me tell you about a guy who dreamed he inherited a million dollars. He dreamed he went to take a shower, but the shower wouldn't shower. He started to shave, but the shaver wouldn't shave. He tried to make some breakfast, but the coffee wouldn't perk, and the toaster wouldn't toast. He went out for the paper, but the paper wasn't there. He waited

What a difference it makes when we get excited about the work we have today!

for the bus, but the bus didn't come. He stood at the stop for forty-five minutes until a guy came puffing down the street. "What's going on around here?" he asked, and the guy gasped, "Haven't you heard? Everybody inherited a million dollars! Nobody's working anymore!"

Just then the man woke up. He had a tremendous shower and a tremendous shave and a tremendous cup of coffee and a tremendous piece of toast. He read a tremendous newspaper and caught a tremendous bus to a tremendous job. What a difference it makes when we get excited about the work we have today!

Many people think enthusiasm or a cheerful spirit is something that falls on you. I want to tell you this with all my heart: the most challenging thing you'll ever face in your life is learning *every day* to be excited about what you're doing.

Sometimes a person says, "I'm preparing for my next job." You had better get excited about the one you've got, or there may not be a next one. Are you excited about what you're doing? This takes *work*. Our work in life is learning to be excited about work. Once you learn a little about enthusiasm on the job, you're on your way.

Once you learn a little about enthusiasm on the job, you're on your way.

THE FIRST FUNCTION OF FOLLOWERSHIP:

Get Excited About Your Work

By: Tracey C. Jones

I get it. It's a big organization, and your part in it is pretty inconsequential. What you do doesn't really matter. In fact, it's beneath you. It's tough to get motivated to do something that nobody even cares about, right?

Wrong!

Let me tell you a secret, one that has taken me years to learn. Every job at every organization is important, or it wouldn't exist. Every employee has the opportunity to contribute in mighty ways, or they might not be employees very long. No organization can exist with dozens of leaders and no followers. Haven't you heard about too many cooks in the kitchen?

You want to be a leader, and that's great. The world needs leaders. But there is more to being a leader than telling people what to do. And there is so much more to learning HOW to lead.

Before you can even think about how great a leader you'll be, you need to be great at doing exactly what you're doing right now. You need to be a team player.

Before you can lead, you need to learn how to follow. That process begins when you make the active decision to get excited about your organization and your part in it.

Yes, leaders must be the loudest cheerleaders of all, but they can't be expected to do everything on their own. What sets any exceptional organization apart isn't just a great leader. It's also a highly motivated team of followers. The truth is, the thing that really excites a leader **is** motivated followers.

Exemplary followers are early adopters of what the leader is trying to accomplish. They honor the leader's goals with their enthusiasm, and that permeates the entire organization. An effective, motivated team is absolutely critical to the leader's or the organization's success. In fact, some scholars state that success is 80% the attitude of the followers and 20% the skills of the leader.

This function might be the most important a follower can embrace. In fact, I was once selected for a job precisely because I was motivated. It was a Project Manager position, and it required a number of years of specific contracting experience that I didn't have. I filled the slot only temporarily, but after six weeks on the job I was given the position permanently. Yes, I demonstrated expertise, but my energy and enthusiasm made the real difference.

We hear a great deal about servant leadership. Well, I am here to tell you, servant followership is just as vital and powerful.

My father used to tell me, "If you want a better job, do a better job, and you'll have a better job."

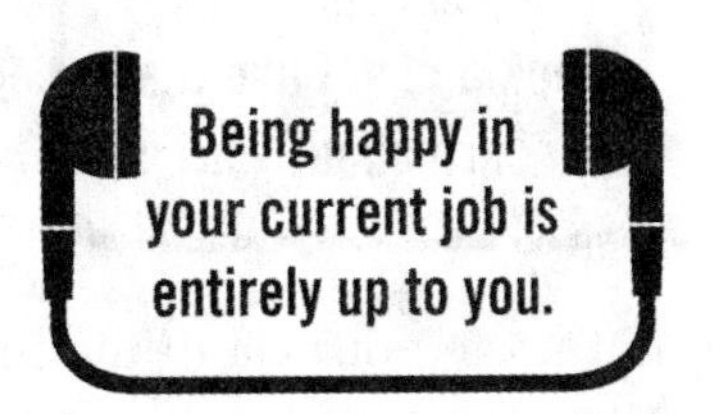

If you can't be happy in your current job, there's a good chance you won't be there for long, and being happy in your current job is entirely up to you. Highly effective followers dial into their own internal cheering section. They find joy in everything they do, even the small, menial tasks. It's all about self-discipline.

Booker T. Washington recommended doing common jobs in uncommon ways. He said, "The cleaning of rooms has a great deal to do with forming one's character." Discipline yourself to serve mightily and cheerfully in small things because when you become a leader, it only gets harder.

If you can't control your attitude in small situations, there is no way you will handle it in the big ones. This makes sense when you realize that the job doesn't make you. You make the job. The more motivated you are, the more tremendous your outcomes.

It really boils down to what type of follower you are. In his book, *The Power of Followership*, Robert Kelley lists five types of followers, from alienated to exemplary. Exemplary followers claim responsibility for their future, their success, and their involvement in the organization. If you won't (not *can't* because that implies it's not up to you) claim the responsibility to be an exemplary follower, you're never going to be an inspirational leader.

> **If you don't look and act like you care, why should anyone look and act like they care about you?**

With whom would you rather work: a happy, motivated, less-than-proficient team member or one who has all the knowledge in the world but a miserable attitude? I can tell you from firsthand experience the one I want on my team.

Let's face it. If you can't come to work and muster a smile and create a positive atmosphere, who will want to be around you? If you don't look and act like you care, why should anyone look and act like they care about you? There's an old saying that your day goes according to the corners of your mouth. I have found this to be a sound truth.

And don't complain at work. Nobody cares if you are unhappy. Misery does not love company. Half of the people you vent to won't care, and the other half are secretly glad something bad is happening to someone other than themselves.

When someone asks you how you are doing at work, just smile and say, –"Tremendous!"—even if you're not. You'll be surprised how much more motivated you start to feel after putting a smile on your face and a positive word on your lips.

Remember this: You are not employed to find happiness. Nowhere in your job description does it say anything about happiness. Once you realize that the greatest benefit you can get from any job, even the crappy ones, is to learn new experiences. Then any job you attack can be approached from a position of excitement. Napoleon Hill, best-selling author of *Think and Grow Rich,* said, "If you're not learning while you're earning, you're missing out on the better part of your compensation." Most of the jobs I held in my early career weren't my "life's passion," but I did them as if they were. Your organization undoubtedly has its share of thumb-sucking freeloaders with sorry attitudes. Choose to be different! You'll make an indelible impression on your organization—for all the right reasons.

Your organization undoubtedly has its share of thumb-sucking freeloaders with sorry attitudes. Choose to be different!

Be proactive. Stay involved at work. Volunteer for projects. Look for solutions before your boss even knows there's a problem, and when you do uncover a problem, deliver a proposed solution to your boss with enthusiasm! Anybody can spot a problem, but the thing that will make you different is your excitement about finding a way to solve it.

Stop asking, "Why did this happen? When will this end? Where did it go wrong?" Those are the questions of a victim. Instead, ask, "How can I be a part of the solution? What can I do to make things better?" Because leaders cannot solve problems without people like you, I guarantee your input will resonate like music to their ears.

Anybody can spot a problem, but the thing that will make you different is your excitement about finding a way to solve it.

The more engaged you stay with your job, the more excitement you generate, (unlike the dead fish who stink up the churning waters of movement and change.)

Also, always remember to finish strong. You will be remembered for how you complete the job, not how you started it, so always stay enthusiastic even if you are planning to put in your two-week notice. When I was in the Air Force, I often witnessed people who announced their retirement and continued to show up for work, but they had checked out of their jobs mentally and emotionally. We described these half-present workers as ROAD, *Retired on Active Duty.* If you are just showing up for work and passively going through the motions, you are ROAD. No leader wants ROAD followers in their organization. Never let an upcoming job change infect your attitude. Finish the race strong.

Excitement about your work is rooted in a heart of gratitude. Seneca said, "Nothing is more honorable than a grateful heart." Learn to be thankful for the job you have right now—there might not be a next one. Treat all work as a privilege. As a follower, you have two choices: You can either work as if you deserve nothing and owe everything, or work as if you deserve everything and owe nothing. One is rooted in gratitude, the other in entitlement. Guess which one will make you stand out as an exemplary follower and put you on the path to becoming a leader? Remember, a great leader must first be a fully developed follower.

Excitement about your work is rooted in a heart of gratitude.

If I am a dependent, I rely on others to meet my needs and to fulfill my happiness. This is most often associated with the years from birth to eighteen. Around eighteen, people should be moving toward a state of independence where they become more and more responsible for taking care of meeting their own needs, physically and emotionally. This step of independence must be mastered before someone can evolve into interdependence, where they meet not only their own needs but also the needs of others. This is the highest form of leadership: a life dedicated to the service of others.

—POINTS TO PONDER—

- There's something in your current job that is going to greatly impact your future success. Find it and work on it.
- Stay away from the water cooler and don't eat lunch in the faculty room. Limit your exposure to gossip and negativity at work.
- When frustrated, always default to humility and remember there are facts and communications you aren't privy to. You don't know what you don't know.
- When upset, step away from the keyboard, take a deep breath, and remember this too shall pass. Anger is one letter away from danger.
- Resist the urge to make a thumb-sucking sympathy call. Your mom will always take your side and you'll only ruin her day.

MILLENNIAL MOMENT #2:

Have you ever said this?

Why should I care? This isn't my dream job!

This "following your dreams" stuff has gone way too far. What if my dreams are to build a Death Star? What if my dreams are to fake my own death and run away from all my responsibilities? You care because it's the adult thing to do. People are depending on you - and paying you - to show up and produce.

You care because it's the right thing to do. If you don't care about your teammates, don't expect them to care about you! Find little ways to enjoy what you are doing. Lighten up and dig in. Be genuinely interested and take pleasure in everything you do. You'll be amazed at how dreamy things suddenly become! If you don't care, you can forget your dream job. It's going to be a nightmare — for you and everyone involved.

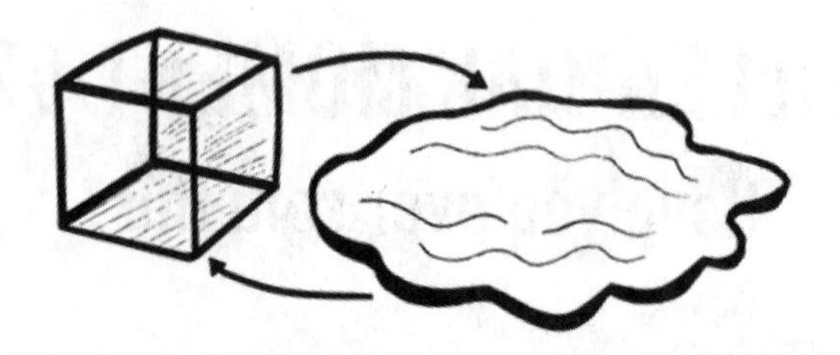

Everything, including you, tends toward a state of disorder unless infused with some type of energy or force. Make the most of what you have today, otherwise tomorrow it will be in a decayed state.

THE SECOND LAW OF LEADERSHIP:

Use or Lose

By: Charlie "Tremendous" Jones

God gives everyone certain attributes, characteristics, and talents, and then He says, "If you use what you have, I'll increase it, but if you don't use it, you'll lose it." Use it or lose it: It's a *law.*

One night, as I came out of a seminar, a fellow confronted me and said, "Charlie, do you think it's possible for a person to be excited, even thrilled, about his work, and be successful in it, but three years later be sick and sorry he ever heard of the whole lousy mess?"

Uh-oh ... another person who doesn't know the law of *Use or Lose.* You see, one day this man was enjoying and using the talent he had. As a result, he was growing and happy. Then, he began to coast, not using what he had, and he began to lose it. One morning he woke up to discover he had failed. Those who lose what they had usually blame the loss on someone else. Consider this: You're never a failure until you blame someone else. As long as you accept the blame for failure, *you* won't be a failure because you're in a position to change the situation.

As long as you accept the blame for failure, you won't be a failure because you're in a position to change the situation.

Let's take a little inventory of our character stock. First, are you multiplying what you already have? Many people are not learning the law of *Use or Lose*. This law says that if you're not using what you have, you're losing it. If you're using what you have, you're getting more of it. For example, some guy asks, "How come I'm twice as smart as she is, but she's making twice as much as I am?" I'll tell you why. She is learning to use what she has, and she's getting more of it.

Check some of the boxes on your character shelf. How's your *Total Commitment?* Have you checked it lately? If you have some, and you've been using it, you're developing more. If you have some and you're not using it, you're losing it.

Now, let's check your *Sincerity*. I don't mean the kind of sincerity you turn on to get your own way. We all know how to act sincere. I'm talking about honest-to-God, genuine sincerity. I'm talking about the kind that grows if you have some and use it but disappears if you have some and don't use it.

Last year I spoke at a national convention of a company in Hollywood Beach, and then I went to see my dad in Pompano Beach. I had just enough time to drive up, tell him I love him, give him a little hug, and then rush away. There wasn't time for lunch, and by the time I stopped for gas I was starved. I thought, "I'll kill two birds with one stone; I'll get gas and run over to the grocery store to get an ice cream sandwich."

I pulled into the gas station and stopped behind another car. As I jumped out, credit card in hand, a fellow meandered over. I said, "Here, take this card and fill my tank. I'll be back in a minute." He replied, "What are you trying to do? Confuse me? What gives?"

My hunger pangs leaped out and snapped: "Take this card and fill this tank or I'll get my gas somewhere else."

I went across the road to get my ice cream sandwich. About halfway there I was struck by a thundering thought: I had just lost a little of my sincerity, and I didn't have much to begin with. I could hardly wait to get back across the street and tell this fellow that I was sorry. When I got back, I said, "Partner, I was rude to you a minute ago, and I want to apologize. I'm sorry." You know what he said? "That's all right. *Everybody's rude to me!*"

One of the greatest things in the world is learning to be a plain, common sense, sincere human being.

Yes, we live in a world where many people thrive on being rude to each other. We know how to act sincere, but we don't know much about *being* sincere. One of the greatest things in the world is learning to be a plain, common sense, sincere human being. If more of us could learn that a little better, maybe our kids would imitate us rather than devastate us.

A person's sincerity is obvious, and it's easy to spot a con man. I can see one a mile away (takes one to know one!). I've discovered that some of the things I resent about others are reflections of my own faults—and I've been more tolerant ever since!

One of the greatest things in the world is for a person who has some sincerity to use it continually with neighbors, family, store clerks, servers. If you're not using that little bit of sincerity you have, you'll lose it. You can't counterfeit or manufacture real sincerity. And what a thrilling thing it is to meet someone who's real and genuinely sincere.

I've discovered that some of the things I resent about others are reflections of my own faults—and I've been more tolerant ever since!

Let's check your *Loyalty* box. A lot of people think loyalty is something you give because of what somebody gave you. That's not loyalty. Loyalty is something you give regardless of what you get back, and in giving loyalty you're getting more loyalty. And out of loyalty flow other great qualities.

Some say, "It'll cost you to be loyal to a family or a company," but consider what it will cost you if you don't use your loyalty. How would you like to belong to an organization where no one is willing to sacrifice for what they believe? You can't change the world, but you can change yourself by using what you have and getting a little more of it. I don't know any way to get loyalty except by using and expanding it.

How's your *Discipline?* There's hardly a thing I hate more than discipline. I've always hated it. I remember my disciplinary dad. Almost every morning he'd say, "Son, this hurts me more than it hurts you." I'd say, "Dad, if it hurts you so much, how come you're always doing it?" I hated discipline.

But later in life I began learning that one of the greatest attributes we can cultivate and multiply is this thing called discipline. Discipline can be multiplied when you submit yourself to authority or a job or a goal. When you submit, you will learn and grow the character trait of discipline.

The person who isn't learning about discipline by being subordinate to authority can try self-discipline, but it'll never work. There is no discipline to apply discipline! If the only person you'll take orders from is yourself, that's not true self discipline. Discipline entails an element of doing what's required by others and not just yourself. Many people fail because they refuse to exercise this essential quality. Even in discouragement and defeat, discipline will spur you to keep constructively busy while you leave behind doubt, worry, and self-pity.

If the only person you'll take orders from is yourself, that's not true self discipline.

Some of us have the attitude "I'll do anything except ..." But in reality, that is the one thing you must do. Discipline springs from taking the difficult challenge and doing what you most despise. You have taken a giant step toward developing a character of discipline when you attempt a job you do not want to do.

You are the only one who can rob your life of character. How? By refusing to make the hard choices. By rejecting the extra time and effort it takes to do the right thing. By accepting less than your best. We will always work against obstacles. There's simply no other way to get more of what you need to do a job well than to use what you have and to do what you can do.

THE SECOND FUNCTION OF FOLLOWERSHIP:

Use or Lose

By: Tracey C. Jones

Thousands of years ago, a wealthy landowner gave bags of gold coins to his three servants for safekeeping before he embarked upon a perilous journey. Upon his return, he summoned his servants to see what they had done with the property that he'd entrusted to them.

The first servant, who was given five bags, used his talents to gain five more. The second, who was given two bags, used his talents to also double the owner's initial investment. The third servant was given a single bag. He was fearful and hid his bag in the earth. Later, he returned the bag to his master, crying, "See, you still have what is yours." The owner cursed him for not working with what he was given, and he threw the servant out into the darkness.

The Parable of the Talents, found in the New Testament, serves as a serious reminder that if we don't use it, we will most certainly lose it. Every talent, tool, resource and benefit entrusted to us needs to be put to good use and multiplied. If we don't do that, we're useless and will be cast out of the organization.

I know it sounds harsh, but that's exactly what the landowner did to the servant who sat on the resources with which he was entrusted. We are engaged and employed by the leader to do conscientious work, to multiply, and to serve a greater good. When we don't, we actually become a liability to our organization.

We are engaged and employed by the leader to do conscientious work, to multiply, and to serve a greater good. When we don't, we actually become a liability to our organization.

Opportunities abound. Some only come around once in a lifetime while others can follow you along your life's journey until you get serious about capturing them. I meet many alienated followers who gripe that they have no opportunities, or that opportunities happen only to others. There's a world of difference between "What opportunities do you have?" and "What opportunities do you *think* you have?" Tell me what you see when you look at this word: OPPORTUNITIESNOWHERE. Do you see *Opportunities Now Here* or *Opportunities No Where?* It's all in how you look at it. How engaged are you as a follower? Do you seize the day or do you seize the excuse?

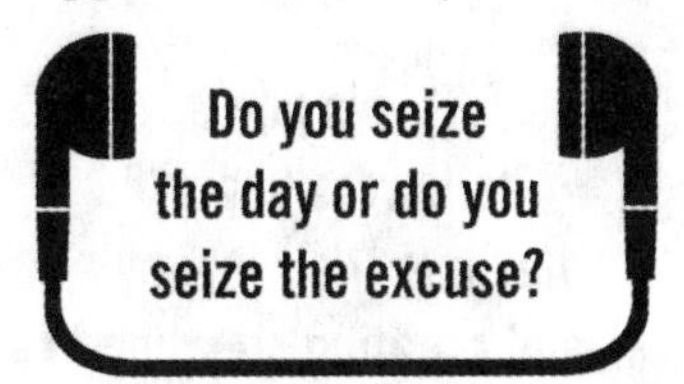

Effective followers seize every opportunity to be a part of something greater than themselves. They are diligent about pouring their resources into the organization through volunteerism and donations or by being an ambassador. Followers are the first ones to value what they've been given and to seek to put those resources to the best possible use. Colonel Sanders said, "There's no use being the richest man in the cemetery. You can't do any business there." Effective followers know that if they don't use it, they will eventually lose it. This is how followers begin building their legacy and creating stepping stones on the path to leadership.

Effective followers seize every opportunity to be a part of something greater than themselves.

All of us have something we can put to good use in this life. Some of us are born into a life of luxury while others are born without even the barest essentials. The fact that we have been given the gift of life means that we are free to turn our situations around at any moment in time. Life throws positive and negative events at us continually. Many of them are outside of our control. But it's not the events that can defeat us. It's how we respond and react to them that determine their outcome. Ineffective followers wander around crying out to the heavens, "Life's not fair" or "When will you give me what I want?" Effective followers know that life is waiting on them to deliver the goods based on their circumstances and their talents. We are free to turn our situations around at any moment in time.

This is how followers begin building their legacy and creating stepping stones on the path to leadership.

Indeed, multiplying what life has given you, even in the most dire of circumstances, is what makes humanity brilliant. In his life-changing book *Man's Search for Meaning*, Holocaust survivor Victor Frankl states, "Ultimately, man should not ask what the meaning of his life is, but rather must recognize that it is he who is asked. In a word, each man is questioned by life; and he can only answer to life by answering for his own life; to life he can only respond by being responsible." If you are reading this, you are already blessed and highly favored. You can read. You can purchase a book. You have the desire to become a more effective leader by becoming a better follower. For you, the sky is the limit. So get out there and get to using before you suffer any more losing!

Back to the Parable of the Talents. I used to think that the owner was too hard on the third servant. After all, he didn't lose anything. He just didn't gain anything. So shouldn't he be given some kind of participation prize for taking the safe route? As I matured, I finally understood the reason for the owner's reaction.

Sitting on what's been given to you does not qualify as creating a legacy or an enhancement.

We are not put on this earth merely to exist and consume precious limited resources. Our purpose in living is to make the world a better place than it was when we got here. Sitting on what's been given to you does not qualify as creating a legacy or an enhancement. We must always search for ways to add value to our lives, our relationships, and our world. As long as you are breathing, you need to be giving back.

My father was not a big fan of retirement. He believed effective followers never retire. The only time we should stop giving is when we stop living!

Volunteerism is most prevalent among two groups of people: those who have just graduated from high school and those who have just left their professional careers. In the first instance, they've got nothing to lose; in the second, they've got nothing to gain. It's critical as followers that we realize the importance of consistently using our talents and spending ourselves to the end of life. Think of the acronym *A.L.I.V.E.:* Always Live In View of Eternity. When you look at life this way, there's never a stopping point.

As long as you are breathing, you need to be giving back.

I'm sure you know some exemplary followers, the ones who are always giving, always volunteering, always busy. Emulate them. It is a universal law that the more you give—the more you get. I remember my father, who was at the time a best-selling author and publisher, telling me that the more free books he gave away, the more money he made.

This is proof positive of the Second Function of Followership: The more we give, the more we get. But if we do not use it, we will most certainly lose it. We all know some people who have lost it, the less-than-exemplary followers. They are the ones who think it's a game to see how little work they can do and still get paid. These alienated followers simply don't realize they aren't hurting the company; they're hurting themselves and their fellow co-workers.

One of my favorite reads with a strong message about engaged followership is *A Message to Garcia* by Elbert Hubbard. Want to learn how to be a top-notch follower? Read this now, and then order one for every member of your team.

> From: *A Message to Garcia*
>
> *If you work for a man, in heaven's name work for him! If he pays you wages that supply you your bread and butter, work for him—speak well of him, think well of him, stand by him and stand by the institution he represents.*
>
> *I think if I worked for a man I would work for him. I would not work for him a part of the time, and the rest of the time work against him. I would give an undivided service or none.*
>
> *If put to the pinch, an ounce of loyalty is worth a pound of cleverness. If you must vilify, condemn and eternally disparage, why, resign your position and, when you are outside, damn to your heart's content. But, I pray you,*

so long as you are a part of an institution, do not condemn it. Not that you will injure the institution—not that—but when you disparage the concern of which you are a part, you disparage yourself.

More than that, you are loosening the tendrils that hold you to the institution, and the first high wind that comes along, you will be up-rooted and blown away in the blizzard's track—and probably you will never know why.

—Elbert Hubbard

—POINTS TO PONDER—

- Remember, if you're not pulling the load, someone in your team has to pick up the slack.
- Your dream job will call your non-dream job for references.
- Finding your dream job takes time. Don't blow your current job just because you don't intend to be here for a long time.
- The organization needs you to do what it's paying you to do. Honor your commitment.
- There is something you can create in your current position that will leave a lasting impression. You leave your legacy everywhere you go; make it a good one!

MILLENNIAL MOMENT #3:
Have you ever said this?

Why don't others see what I'm capable of?

There is a stark difference between strategy and tactics, and you have a tough time discerning the difference. Your big picture involves winning the lottery and changing the world, but you haven't figured out that hope is not a strategy.

There is a big difference between the coach and the quarterback, and it's a difference that seems lost on too many young people entering the work force. You have dreams and aspirations. Great. But the simple truth is, your boss probably doesn't care about those. Your boss just wants the job done.

The only way to show others what you're capable of is to actually SHOW them. That means less talking and more doing. Don't tell your employer how to move the ball forward.

Pick it up and move it forward. Because that's the only way it's going to move.

There's a reason talk is cheap; it doesn't accomplish anything. Get your action plans in place and start producing results. And don't worry if you make a mistake. Trust me, you're going to have plenty of failures along the way. Don't worry. Failure is just nature's way of showing the world how hard you're working and trying.

Life is so much more navigable when you are already in motion. If you don't know what to do next, just do something. A ship can only change course when it is in motion.

THE THIRD LAW OF LEADERSHIP:

Production to Perfection

By: Charlie "Tremendous" Jones

Once in a while I meet someone who says, "You know, I don't believe in leaving a job half completed and poorly done. When I do something, it's got to be perfect."

Have you heard about Sam's Clothing Store? Sam was quite a guy. He knew about the law of Production to Perfection. One day John came in to see Sam. He said, "Sam, I want to buy a suit."

Sam said, "S-h-h!"

John said, "What d'ya mean, s-h-h?"

"We don't sell suits here."

"Then what are all these things?"

Sam whispered, "Well, uh, when you come in here to buy a suit, it's not here. Walk over this way. It's not as if we could sell you one off the rack. When you come in here to buy a suit, it's a project! We make it an event. We've got to know the real you. We've got to know your attitude and your aptitude, your likes and your dislikes. And when we get to know the real you, we pick the right wool that fits you. We even go to England to pick the right sheep that fits you. And the silk lining—we go to Japan to get the right silk; we even pick out the right worm. And the buttons? We go to Alaska to pick the elk that fits you."

"Wait a minute, Sam. I've got to have a suit today!"

Sam purred, "You'll have it."

Now, I believe in doing things right. In fact, one of my frequent prayers, the cry of my heart, is "O God, let me do one thing right before I die." But I add, "In the meantime, Lord, help me do *something!*"

There's a law that says, if you're not learning to make something happen today, you won't know much about perfection tomorrow. As a young salesman, I learned this every step of the way. As a husband, father, Sunday school teacher, you name it, my heart delighted in doing something because while it might have been better had I waited a little longer, many of those somethings might not otherwise have been done at all.

There is a plague sweeping the world, and it's reaching epidemic proportions. It's the Quitter's Disease. Everywhere I go I hear the phrase, "I QUIT!" Every time I return to the office, I expect to be greeted by some overwhelmingly unhappy associate and a great big "I QUIT!"

The problem with most of us is that we don't fully realize and understand ourselves. I always wanted to quit whatever job I held. In fact, that's why I worked so hard to become successful. I thought that success would eliminate my agonizing desire to quit all the time. Then, finally, I became a success, and, to my surprise, I wanted to quit anyway. That's when I learned that the human mind hits psychological lows two or three times a year, and it wants to quit for no reason at all.

That's when I learned that the human mind hits psychological lows two or three times a year, and it wants to quit for no reason at all.

Of course, the real problem wasn't the job as much as it was simply *wanting* to quit. The more I wanted to quit, the more the desire to quit dominated my mind. The more I wanted to quit, the more I was afraid I was *going* to quit. I didn't really want to quit. I just wanted to *want* to quit. One day I discovered the difference between quitting and wanting to quit, and I decided that I would *never* quit. Now I enjoy quitting all the time because *I know I'm not going to QUIT*.

Often someone will ask, "You mean a good worker and a good follower can't ever quit?" That's right. You can die, retire, or get fired, but that's it. Of course, there are exceptions, and you are going to think you're the exception every time you want to quit, but if you sell out that easily, you'll never get to pay the first price of leadership. I think you'll agree that more is to be gained by stickability than by chasing better deals. Most of the time quitting sets the stage for almost certain failure in your next venture.

Most of the time quitting sets the stage for almost certain failure in your next venture.

Instead of cultivating an urge to quit, we should cultivate a sense of urgency about our work. I believe that the fires of inspiration and greatness in our hearts can be kept burning only by developing a sense of urgency and importance in our work—not the work I'm going to do, not the work I wish I could do, but the work I am doing *now.*

A sense of urgency informs you that yesterday is gone forever, and tomorrow may never come, but today is in your hands. Urgency convicts you that shirking today's work will add to tomorrow's burden; it helps you accomplish the task that today sets before you.

Thank God for the sense of urgency that changes a dull, menial job into a sparkling career. A sense of urgency is not the complete solution, but it is a tremendous step in the right direction. Whatever your work is, if you don't have a sense of urgency about it, ask God for help. Believe that He will answer your prayer and then act accordingly. Rather than wandering through life looking for something that never existed, develop a sense of urgency and begin to live.

Thank God for the sense of urgency that changes a dull, menial job into a sparkling career.

THE THIRD FUNCTION OF FOLLOWERSHIP:

Production to Perfection

By: Tracey C. Jones

We've all heard the Nike slogan "Just Do It." That's how I'd describe the Third Function of Followership. You may ask, "Just do what, Tracey?" My response is: *Anything!* Just do something. Trust me, sitting and contemplating what to do is not going to put you on any track to leadership. General George S. Patton said something intriguing: "A poor plan, violently executed now, is better than a perfect plan next week." How can that be, you ask? Because Patton understood the Third Function of Followership: Nobody ever gets it right the first time. Starting is the hardest part. The only way we truly learn is through experience.

Southwest Airlines CEO Herb Kelleher put it simply. "We have a strategic plan," he said. "It's called doing things."

To be an effective follower, you need to keep your eye on the goal and adjust the moves you make as necessary. Perhaps you aren't being given the production positions you want right now. That's okay. Find the need, and dig in. Don Hodel, who served as Secretary of Energy and Secretary of the Interior before leaving public life to lead Focus on the Family, was known to offer this advice, "Do the needful." But remember this: Just because you want to do something that you think is needed, it may not be in the best interest or timing for your organization. Discuss with your supervisors what your short and long-range plans are so they are aware of what you are planning for your future. They will appreciate your openness. Leaders can't read minds even though followers get frustrated and act like they can.

Leaders can't read minds even though followers get frustrated and act like they can.

In *The Tipping Point,* Malcolm Gladwell states that it takes approximately 10,000 hours to achieve mastery in any field. Production to Perfection takes time. It does not come with a degree or a job title. When I pinned on my lieutenant bars, I clearly understood that for the next four years I was in training as a junior officer. I hadn't seen enough nor done enough to warrant any huge fanfare. I wasn't there to produce results. I was in this early phase to *learn how to produce results*. It takes a good deal of seasoning to produce perfection.

A basic part of learning to produce results is taking your work seriously. Don't merely look at the completion of tasks as a compliance-oriented step, but rather make a covenant with the organization and with yourself to do the best job that you can. Some people do the same job for twenty years and call it a career. Others stretch out of their comfort zones and move closer to the new definition of perfection each and every year. Guess which type of follower your leader wants you to be? Guess which type of follower is more likely to become a leader? Leaders want a follower who doesn't just produce results. They want a follower who creates a new exemplary standard within the organization. Production to perfection means you have a deeply vested interest in every moment you spend in the organization. You take this commitment seriously while some others may have

Make a covenant with the organization and with yourself to do the best job that you can.

no qualms about taking advantage of the organization and the system. That's what sets the exemplary follower apart.

Many people in an organization become miserable and unhappy when they expect everything to go right and it doesn't. Character is built in such difficulties and disappointments. Iron is sharpened and diamonds are cut in the fire and pressure of circumstances. It takes time and resilience to move along the path to perfection. Two construction workers sat down to eat their lunches one day. One worker opened his lunch box, took out the sandwich, and exclaimed, "Oh no, not peanut-butter sandwiches!" The next day, the exact same thing happened. This went on for several more days before his co-worker finally said, "Joe, if you don't like peanut-butter sandwiches, just tell your wife not to pack them anymore!" His friend fired back, "You leave my wife out of this. *I pack my own lunch!*" So what are you packing in your lunch pail? The same old peanut-butter every day? Or are you cooking up something worthy of a five-star rating?

Iron is sharpened and diamonds are cut in the fire and pressure of circumstances.

A tremendous book every exemplary follower should read is *Good to Great* by Jim Collins. Collins argues that the difference between good and great is sustained long-term performance. Sure sounds like the Third Function of Followership. If you can't bring your production to perfection, why bother? What's the point of stepping up to the plate if you don't eventually hope to hit it out of the park? Collins outlines the Hedgehog Concept which can help every follower determine their greatest skills and traits by asking three questions of the reader: *What are you deeply passionate about? In what skills can you excel?* And *what drives your economic engine?* When you dial into the intersection of these three questions, you will find your production coming to perfection.

Remember, followership isn't just about producing results. It's about *perfecting* results. This happens as a result of the conscientiousness and discipline of the follower. In *The New Common Denominator of Success*, Albert E.N. Gray states that the only difference between failure and success is that success has made a habit of doing the things that failure doesn't like to do. It's that simple!

And it's that hard. Forming a habit takes self-discipline, the only form of discipline that lasts. Self-discipline and self-motivation are what will determine how closely you develop this particular function of followership. The other functions may rely on enthusiasm or risk, but this one is all about true grit and stickability.

Production to Perfection is about how followers express themselves in their habits. Do you have a habit of following through on assignments? Do you have personal accountability? Or have you built a reputation of dropping the ball or passing the buck? Do you have a habit of always searching for better ways to produce results, or are you obsessed with finding excuses? Do you have a habit of employing critical-thinking skills so you can get clarity on the true issues at hand, or do you blindly listen to office gossip or the media?

> **Inch by inch,
> life's a cinch;
> yard by yard,
> life is hard**

Aristotle said, "We are what we repeatedly do. Excellence, then, is not an act, but a habit."

Inch by inch, life's a cinch; yard by yard, life is hard. Perfection is acquired one small step at a time. Every day, make the commitment to do one thing that will move you closer to your ideal of perfection. At the end of the year, you'll be 365 habits closer than you are right now!

An old adage states, "Unless you're the lead dog, the scenery never changes." But for the exemplary follower, the scenery is always changing as paths are forged from production to perfection. Make sure you take every chance to bloom where you are planted because each of these seasons—every crappy job—serves to deepen your root structure. Diverting your critical resources to the most important task will prune your skills and give you the chance to grow. The result will be an unimaginable depth of character, motivation, and discipline. Be prepared to surprise yourself.

—POINTS TO PONDER—

- What are you doing to show others your capabilities and your accomplishments?
- Remember, it takes time to build your reputation.
- First, get the job done. Then worry about credit.
- Celebrate your successes, even if nobody else does.
- Take responsibility for your own self-esteem. Know in your heart you did the best you can do.

MILLENNIAL MOMENT #4:
Have you ever said this?

What's in it for me?

The fact is you have no idea how you are going to grow or be challenged until you begin actually doing something. In our day, "the satisfaction of a job well done" was enough to keep us motivated. And, let's face it, some things on the to-do list are not at all intrinsically motivating. But they need doing, and you're the one tasked with getting them done.

There's something beautifully simplistic and satisfying in accomplishing the task at hand. In the military, we called anything we really didn't want to do "good training" because we knew it had to be done, so we may as well learn something in the process.

You want to change the world, and the task before you probably isn't going to get you there. I get it. But I hope you get that the only way you're going to change the world is if you change yourself. That means getting your heart in line with thinking of others before yourself. Simply put, that's accomplished one task at a time. Spend less time thinking of what you're going to get out of it and more time focused on how your efforts impact the lives of others.

The greatest commandment in the world is to love others. The greatest unifying force in the world is love. All of humanity is one vast love story. Life is all about loving others.

THE FOURTH LAW OF LEADERSHIP:

Give to Get

By: Charlie "Tremendous" Jones

"I really believe that law," someone says. "My granddad taught me that. And my wife says it, too. And just last week the pastor preached on it. He said, 'If you give, you'll get!'"

Don't you believe it! It's not true.

Have you heard of the guy who said, "Well, my secret of success is: I gave. Yes, I gave and gave and gave and gave" (and his demeanor silently adds, "and look at all I got").

People who give to get would be better off if they didn't get anything. Some people have been ruined by what they got because they didn't get what they thought they were going to get—it *got them,* and there's a difference!

True leadership is learning to give whether you receive anything or not! If you give finances, time, help or anything in order to get something, *you're not giving* in the true sense of the word. *You're trading!*

Many people know very little about true, sacrificial giving without the hope of getting anything in return. One of the great problems in marriage today is the inability of some partners to give without expecting anything in return. We know so little about giving, but we know all about trading.

We know so little about giving, but we know all about trading.

If you *learn to give, despite the fact that you may get nothing in return,* you have learned true giving. The act of giving without any hope of recompense creates a greater capacity to give in the giver. This increasing capacity forms a ready reservoir for a marketable commodity, no matter what the bank account says. This will always enable you to produce and give and to live confidently and securely in a world that's running scared.

You may lose your reputation, your home, and even your family, but you can never lose your capacity to give *if you're learning to give.* But *you're not really giving* if you give to get something other than a greater capacity to give.

Once a fellow said to me, "You know why I can't work six days a week, twenty hours a day?"

"Why?" I asked.

"Because this isn't my business. If this were my own business, boy, I could put out! But I have no proprietary interest here. If it were something I could leave to my kids, I'd work night and day. I'd…"

Wait a minute. I worked sixteen years for a company where I drew a paycheck. In those sixteen years I didn't work one day for that company. For whom was I working? I was working for Charles E. Jones and his six little bread-snappers! There were many times when I knew I was giving my best to the company, and I wasn't getting anything except heartaches, misery and problems on problems. But I was aware I was learning to give in the truest sense.

The young contractor who married a contractor's daughter had to learn the hard way. The father-in-law wanted to give a boost to his new son-in-law.

"Son," he said, "I don't want you to start at the bottom where I did. So I want you to go out and build the most tremendous house this town has ever seen, put the best of everything in it, make it a palace, and turn it over to me."

Well, this was an opportunity to make a killing. He hurried out to slap together a building that would survive two fairly stiff gales. In short order, he was back to dear old dad. "Well, Dad, it's finished."

"Is it tremendous? Is it a palace?"

"Yes siree, Dad."

"Is it really the finest house ever built, son?"

"Yes siree, Dad."

"All right, where is the bill? Is there a good profit in it for you?"

"Yes siree, Dad."

"Very good. Here is your check. Where is the deed?"

As he looked at the deed, the father said, "I didn't tell you why I wanted that house to be the best house ever built. I wanted to do something special for you and my daughter to show you how much I love you. Here, take the deed, go live in the house. You built it for yourself!"

The young goldbricker crept out, a shattered, frustrated man. He thought he was making a fortune at his father-in-law's expense by saving money on inferior materials and short-cuts, but he cheated only himself.

A better life rises from an increasing capacity to give.

Contractor or not, you're building a life. A better life rises from an increasing capacity to give. Real giving makes real living, creating a capacity to give something that no one else can.

I want to assure you that the person hasn't lived who practiced this law to its fullest potential. There's not a man, including myself, who knows much about giving. But by the grace of God, anyone can be doing a better job of learning the law of *Give to Get.* And remember, what you get is not a return gift but a greater capacity to go beyond where you are. That's a law for growing.

THE FOURTH FUNCTION OF FOLLOWERSHIP:

Give to Get

By: Tracey C. Jones

This is a tough one. We often give our best because we expect to be rewarded with increased responsibility, pay, or job titles. While this is completely understandable, true followership has to be rooted in the Fourth Function of Followership which is grounded in *obedience.* We do what is expected of us, and we serve beyond our duty and to the utmost of our capability because that is what truly defines our character. We serve with the expectation of nothing in return, except the joy of fulfilling our mission.

That's right, I said joy. Sometimes, as a follower, that's all you're going to get in return: the personal satisfaction of a job done well.

When we give, we have to do it with a joyful heart. We cannot give because we feel obligated. In the grand scheme of things, we entered this world with nothing, and we will leave it with nothing. In essence, what we are doing when we give is just returning some of what has been given to us.

If you give to get something in return, you are declaring to the world that your self-interest matters, but the simple fact is, it doesn't. As my father used to say, if you give to get, that's not giving; it's trading. The heart of a giving follower finds purpose in helping others, regardless of what's in it for him or her.

Heda Bejar commented beautifully: "The fragrance always remains in the hand that gives the rose." There are four paths we can take in life. We can lash out at perceived injustices and seek revenge; we can throw in the towel and seek seclusion; we can drift through life blissfully unaware; or we can work to pour our lives into others.

When we give to *give* and not *get,* we receive a number of benefits. Serving elevates the follower. Serving corrects our focus and clears our lenses so we can see clearly. Serving has tremendous educational benefits.

We've been taught that nice guys finish last, that if you give someone an inch, they'll take a mile, that we are not to let others treat us like door mats. It's a dog-eat-dog world, and you better be the top dog. These ideas are completely false. When you perform as a servant follower, you are giving and gaining respect.

I'm reminded of the story of *The Sheep Thief,* which takes place in a small Italian village several hundred years ago. Two young men were caught stealing sheep. They were branded with an "ST" on their foreheads, declaring to everyone who they were and what they had done. The first young man was so angry and ashamed that he fled the town. He wandered endlessly until he died, alone and broke. The second young man was determined to change his reputation and become a giver. He stayed in the town, got a job, and worked until he was able to pay back the man whose sheep he had stolen. Then he built a business that employed many townsfolk. He was generous and active in his community. Many years later a stranger came through and saw this benevolent pillar of the community. He asked a nearby shop keeper what the "ST" on the old man's forehead represented.

The shopkeeper, knowing full well the entire story, stopped for a minute to think and then replied, "Saint."

The meaning of life is to live a life of meaning, and that's really what most of us want to do. We want to matter. Unfortunately, too many of us believe that the only way to make a difference in the world is to become a leader because only leaders can affect the world. This is simply not true.

Once you realize that life is about sowing the seeds, not reaping the harvest, you'll begin to understand that true leadership starts with exemplary followership. All of us, leaders or not, should seek to serve in any way possible and to the best of our ability.

Remember, if serving is below you, leading is beyond you. Zig Ziglar said, "The best way to get what you want is to help enough other people get what they want." Time and time again, the most miserable people I see are the ones who are solely focused on themselves and what they can get out of life. We live in a world that is obsessed with vanity and self-absorption. Growing up, I was told that if I gazed at myself in the mirror too long I was conceited. Today, the internet is filled to the brim with "selfies." People put themselves out there for the public view, just to draw more attention to themselves. This most certainly is a flawed focus for a follower.

Whether you realize it or not, there are intrinsic benefits from giving to give. One benefit is the tremendous education that results, simply by learning to be an effective follower, especially in a world where people seem determined to take from one another. Serving develops not just your mind but also your heart. Giving to give grounds you in truth, not just in rewards.

Serving develops not just your mind but also your heart. Giving to give grounds you in truth, not just in rewards.

Many people only respond to rewards, an indication of shallow, self-centered attitudes. No leader can work with a follower who is only motivated by rewards. An astute leader knows that a self-centered follower will be gone the second they believe the grass is greener elsewhere. These followers are mere mercenaries, always looking for a better payoff.

Serving creates a more gentle, sympathetic, and compassionate person. Often, the folks who scream the loudest about inequalities in the world are the ones who give the least. The most significant thing a follower can do is to stop pointing out what is wrong and questioning why something is happening. A good follower will try to be a proactive part of the solution. Giving creates generosity and a sweet spirit. Giving enables the follower to see beauty in an ugly world.

I'm reminded of the story of two men in hospice care. Neither was able to sit up on his own, but one man was propped up for one hour a day during his treatments. During this time, he would look out the window by the bed and describe the wonders of the outside world to his suitemate. This was the highlight of the other man's day. When the man by the window died, the second man asked if he could have his friend's bed by the window. When he first sat in the bed, he leaned over and pulled back the drape. To his surprise, all he saw was a brick wall. The man was shocked and asked the nurse why his friend had lied by describing something that wasn't there. The nurse explained that the man was actually blind, but he had attempted to brighten his friend's day with his beautiful descriptions of the scene outside the window.

Giving enables the follower to see beauty in an ugly world.

We should give, not to get in return, but to better the lives of others. This is the only thing that matters in the life of a follower, or, when you think about it, a leader. We all have a soul hole, but when we seek to serve others, we make our own soul whole.

—POINTS TO PONDER—

- Be grateful for what you have in the moment.
- The opportunity to grow and learn is the greatest reward of all.
- It's not only about you. Find a way to support and empower others.
- The timeline between sowing and reaping is always longer than you think.

MILLENNIAL MOMENT #5:
Have you ever said this?

I don't know how to do that.

You are part of the generation that can find out anything in the entire universe with the touch of your finger. But you've lost something along the way. You are a passive recipient of information, not a critical thinking problem solver. It's only natural when you've been exposed to so much technology and so many channels at an early age.

As a rule, when quantity rises, quality declines. You must take the initiative and weed through all the data and start figuring things out for yourself. Don't allow yourself to become lazy in your thinking. There's a ton of research in mental plasticity. Thinking is a perishable skill. The less you do it, the harder it's going to be to get back in the habit.

Every experience we have
delivers another key with
which to open a door to life.
The more keys you have,
the more doors you can open.
Fill up your key ring with
every type of experience,
good, bad and ugly.

THE FIFTH LAW OF LEADERSHIP:

Exposure to Experience

By: Charlie "Tremendous" Jones

In the beginning of life, God gives every person a psychological key ring. And He gives a law that says, "Every time you expose yourself to a new situation, I'll give you another key of experience for your key ring."

Soon the key ring begins to fill with experiences, and we learn to pick the right key to unlock any situation. The person who doesn't learn the law of *Exposure to Experience* fumbles around trying to find a key that he doesn't have, or maybe he has it somewhere but he wastes time trying to find it because he hasn't been using it. Then, when he finally finds the key, somebody else has come along and taken home the bacon.

Sometimes the fellow who gets lots of bacon decides to relax and enjoy it. By the time he reaches forty or forty-five, his income has spiraled up steadily. This living success story says, "It's about time I slow down and enjoy my reward."

Trouble!

What makes a person really produce? It's knowing that he owes life a considerable amount, and he deserves little. But when a person reaches the place where he thinks, "I don't owe anything to anyone, and I deserve a lot," he's heading downhill.

One of the biggest lies ever palmed off on mankind is "Success is a reward to be enjoyed." I don't know one person who uses success as a reward and is genuinely happy. Luke 12:48 reminds us, to whom much is given, much shall be required. Luke 12:48 Success is not a reward to be enjoyed but a trust to be administered.

Success is not a reward to be enjoyed but a trust to be administered.

I know people around the country who could go fishing for the rest of their days, but instead they choose to stay dynamically active. And they're having the time of their lives.

This is an exciting law because its practice makes things get better and better as the years go by. As you accumulate experiences, you use those keys over and over again. Eventually, you know which keys to use to unlock certain doors, and you slip through with ease while the inexperienced people search feverishly to see if they even have a key. The old-timer who learns the law of *Exposure to Experience* doesn't need the stamina that he once needed; he knows how to get to the heart of a problem and prescribe a remedy.

The most dynamic, tremendous people who have impacted my life through the years have been over sixty years old. Some are over seventy, and last year the man whose life excited me the most was over eighty!

Many people who are getting old waste time wishing they were young again. I don't wish I were young again. I had plenty of fun. The young are miserable with unanswered questions—at least *I* was. Look at some of these dynamic old geezers. Their exuberance could ruin the Senior Citizen Program. I'm convinced that practicing the law of *Exposure to Experience* can make every year of your life more fulfilling than the last.

The young are miserable with unanswered questions—at least *I* was.

It's a shame that people *get* old rather than *grow* old. A person who *gets* old is not practicing the law of *Exposure to Experience.* Getting old means you're drifting not growing, and that means getting shallow and cynical and thankless. But if you *grow* old, life will become deeper, richer, and fuller. It's exciting to grow old as you practice the law of *Exposure to Experience.*

This law has absolutely no short cuts. You have to take the main route through all the traffic, but it gets you where you want to go.

There's no way to learn this law of experience other than through exposure. I didn't get much business in my early days, but I sure had plenty of exposure, and that exposure gave me experience that eventually landed a ton of business for me.

This law has absolutely no short cuts. You have to take the main route through all the traffic, but it gets you where you want to go.

THE FIFTH FUNCTION OF FOLLOWERSHIP:

Exposure to Experience

By: Tracey C. Jones

I am reminded of the story of a young man who asked a seasoned CEO how he became so successful. The CEO replied, "Good judgment." The young man, anxious to learn more, pressed further, asking how to acquire good judgment. The CEO replied, "Experience." Exasperated, the young man asked how to get experience, to which the CEO replied, *"Poor judgment."*

If you're laughing at this story, you know what I mean. This analogy used to scare me. Now I embrace it because I understand the sweet truth behind it.

One of my favorite lines is "The quickest way to success is to cram fifty years of failure into fifteen." Fail early, fail often, and fail forward. Does this mean that you try to foul-up your opportunities? Absolutely not! It means you embrace each new chance to act, and whether you win or lose, it's about doing your best and moving up the ladder of exposure to experience.

If you find followership or leadership easy, you're doing it wrong.

Let's face it. You are never going to meet a strong person who has had an easy past. If you find followership or leadership easy, you're doing it wrong.

When I was growing up, my father would always tell me I had to "earn my stripes." This meant I had to go out and find my own path and not stay hidden in his shadow. Success by association is a myth. You have to go out and earn it yourself, not merely rub shoulders with successful people. I can remember my father's joke about the man who burst into his office shouting, "I QUIT!" My father said, "You can't quit! *You haven't done anything yet!*"

Success by association is a myth.

As my father stated, we are all born with an empty key ring, and every experience, good, bad, and ugly, gives us another key to hang on that ring. The more experiences you have, the more keys you accumulate. As you grow older and become more seasoned, you'll realize that no matter what door you face, you probably have the key that unlocks it.

As a follower, the more risks you take, the more you venture out of your comfort zone. The more times you stand up and say, "I will," while everyone else looks at the table, the more keys you will have to unlock the unlimited doors ahead of you.

Sure, you're going to encounter failure, but do you know the only true way a follower grows? It's by failure. Adversity isn't a noble thing, but it is a character-building thing. And the most important thing a follower can do on the path to leadership is to develop character.

Adversity isn't a noble thing, but it is a character-building thing.

Every day, we have to unlearn and relearn what we thought we already knew. W. Edwards Deming said, "Learning is not compulsory; neither is survival." Effective followers realize that they must be in a continuous learning mode for the rest of their lives. The path to success is covered with obstacles and regressions that only persistence and an embrace of experience will get you through.

Every day, we have to unlearn and relearn what we thought we already knew.

It took me seven years to complete an undergraduate degree and four different careers over the span of three decades before I finally landed where I was supposed to be. What can I say. I'm a late bloomer! Was anything I did a waste of time? Did I regret not achieving clarity sooner? Do I beat myself up for being so slow? Absolutely not!

Remember, not all who wander are lost. Some of us are just filling up our key ring until we figure out what we were put on this Earth to do. Because of my wealth of experiences, I can talk with any leader from any business and recognize what they are going through. How? Because I've personally lived it. I haven't just read about it. It's experiential and instinctive for me.

Effective followers realize that they must be in a continuous learning mode for the rest of their lives.

As a well-seasoned follower, you can offer your leaders a wealth of experiential knowledge. In addition, be sure that you expose yourself to the experiences of the great minds who have gone before. In other words, read great books. You don't have enough time to make all the mistakes, profit from all the failures, and earn all the stripes on your own. Read profusely about how the greats of the past dealt with their individual challenges.

Even if promotion is impossible in your position, you can still be an active follower by investing in personal research and development. One of the beneficial assets of technology is accessibility to the most powerful and effective speeches of the greatest minds in history. Take advantage of that. Don't wait for someone to tell you how to use and profit from internet use. Figure it out on your own. Expose yourself to the experiences of others.

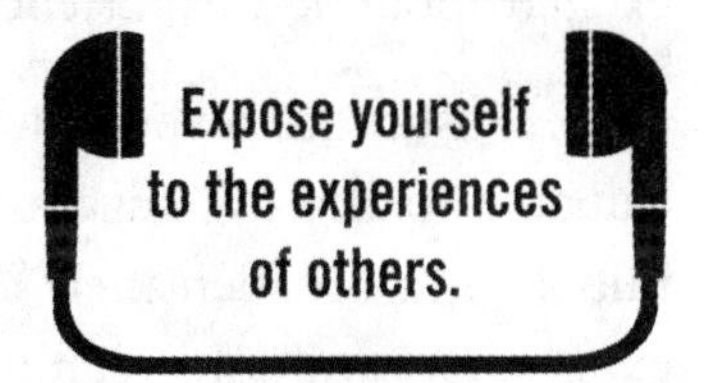

Experiences, like opportunities, abound. Experiences can morph into opportunities. The question is whether or not you choose to expose yourself to those experiences. Effective followers won't stop there. Exemplary followers will be chomping at the bit to try new experiences and challenges.

In his book *The Power of Followership*, Robert Kelley lists the qualities of exemplary followers. He writes that followers focus on goals, do a great job on critical-path activities related to the goal, and take the initiative to increase their value to the organization. Kelley recommends having a personal conversation with your leader to see how you can better achieve the organization's goals. This will mean exposing yourself to new experiences. Leaders love followers who are excited about new experiences.

Leaders love followers who are excited about new experiences.

Exposure to experience also makes followers more valuable to the organization because they have taken the initiative to broaden their careers. A follower with various experiences will understand multiple facets of the company because of their exposure to various areas. In several of my career fields, both civilian and military, there were programs where employees would rotate through the various areas of the organization, spending a short time in each one. This meant we had to understand how each section contributed to the mission, and it connected us with our fellow team members to create a higher degree of collaboration. It also enabled us to take anyone's place should the need arise.

Experience can make you an indispensable follower, so don't be a one-trick pony.

Another benefit of wide experience within the organization is the premium placed on your abilities. You can become invaluable to its functioning. The more you can do for the organization, the greater your longevity will be as the business goes through unavoidable changes in structure and economics that happen everywhere. Experience can make you an indispensable follower, so don't be a one-trick pony. Get as much experience as you can.

—POINTS TO PONDER—

- Before you ask for help, try three times to figure it out and overcome the obstacle(s).
- If it's a pervasive problem in the organization, develop a resource for others.
- The more you know the more you grow.
- Develop a healthy relationship with failure. The sooner you get all the failures out of the way the quicker you can move onto the successes.

MILLENNIAL MOMENT #6:
Have you ever said this?

Why wasn't I selected?

How self-aware are you? Can you be objective with yourself? Would *you* hire *you*? Do you surround yourself with people who tell you what you need to hear and not what you want to hear? It's the old plank-in-the-eye syndrome. We—all of us—have the hardest time spotting our own weaknesses.

If you really want to know why you weren't picked, ask your boss. But do so with an open mind and a genuine interest in the answer. Do you have a cadre of people who can have honest conversations with you? If not, you're never going to become what you could be.

Not getting what you want teaches humility. There is tremendous value in learning patience. Often, not getting what you want now turns out to be a blessing in disguise down the road, because something you need to improve upon or change now will make a tremendous difference later. If you're willing.

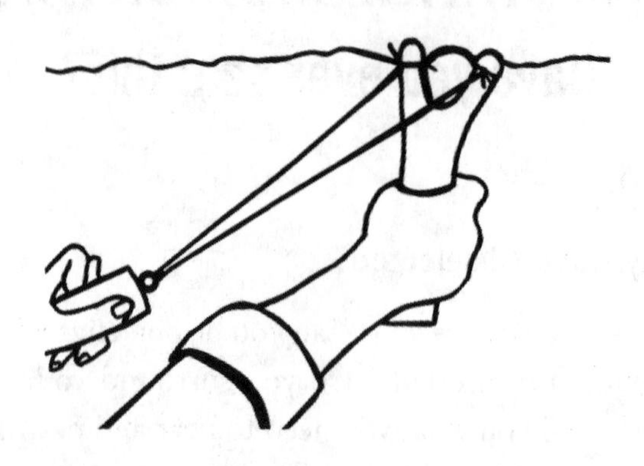

The more we get set back, the greater the tension to fly forward when we are released. Allow the mistakes and bumps that set you back to catapult you to your future successes.

THE SIXTH LAW OF LEADERSHIP:

Flexible Planning

By: Charlie "Tremendous" Jones

This is the age of the planner, the organizer. At seminars we hear dynamic lecturers say, "Show me someone who plans, and I'll show you a success." I say, "Show me someone who says that, and I'll show you an idiot."

Don't ever think that planning will do it. I used to plan the plans to end all plans, and I almost planned myself out of business a half-dozen times. Planning can't be the answer.

You've heard the sad sack who moans, "I'm no quitter. I've tried six plans, but I'm not quitting yet. I'm making one more plan. If this plan doesn't work, I've had it." I've got news for him. He's had it already.

Now, I believe in planning, but the key is *Flexible Planning*. Have a plan—a flexible one.

Flexible Planning allows for the fact that *whatever can go wrong—will go wrong*. And since we know that whatever can go wrong may go wrong at the wrong time, *Flexible Planning* says, plan on your plan going wrong so that you're ready with an alternate plan because *"That's my plan!"*

Many people are miserable because they expect everything to go right. They're *asking* for misery. Instead, I expect things to go wrong, so I'm jubilant whenever they go right. A smart guy asked me, "What if something goes right?" Easy: I can work it in. I haven't had much trouble with that yet.

Try this tomorrow morning. Say, "Lord, send me some miserable problems today." I've done it, and no sooner did my day begin, and I found myself saying, "You sure answered that prayer in a hurry." Perhaps you don't have to pray such a prayer because the miserable problems come anyway. The key is: Are you prepared for them?

When I entered the life insurance business, someone from the company explained the product and provided sales training. I could hardly wait to get out in the field. Finally, the big day came, and I asked the manager, "To whom do I sell?" He said, "The world is your market!" The whole world. What an opportunity!

But I was disorganized. I was like that Texan who rushed into the airport and demanded, "Gimme a ticket!"

"Where to?" asked the agent, fumbling with the tickets.

The Texan trumpeted, "It doesn't matter. I've got business *all over!*"

Talk about confusion! I was the master of it. When something went wrong, I would jump in my car, race to the manager's office, and say, "I've got a problem." And he'd say, "Let me tell you what it is. Your problem is planning." I thought, "Oh, is he smart! I didn't even tell him the problem, and he gave me the answer." That routine satisfied me until the twentieth time. Then, I realized my approach to the customer was a canned sales talk. You know the trouble with canned sales talks? The customers don't know their parts.

Those who are growing understand that things go wrong to make us more right.

We need to learn *Flexible Planning*. Those who are growing understand that things go wrong to make us more right.

God only breaks us down with problems so He can build us back up again.

The wild stallion may look beautiful on the mesa with his mane blowing in the wind, but he isn't much use until somebody breaks him so he can pull a load or carry a rider. Neither is a person much good until harnessed to teamwork and disciplined to guidance. God trains us so we can run free. That's an old law; you can fight it, but you'll never change it. Imagine how superficial our lives would be if God didn't send circumstances that seem disastrous but later prove to be enriching and meaningful.

One of my employees told me, "I'm going to have to quit." I asked him why. "Well, I don't think this is God's will for me. Things are awful."

"They're awful?" I said. "That means you're right where you ought to be. This can make you a success!"

I'll never forget the big policy I sold after I'd been in the business three years. We built a big, beautiful home on the profits. But sometimes things get confused in pension cases, and this one was the confusion of all confusions. Finally, I had to give all my earnings back, and I was stuck with that fancy home.

That's always been the way with me. So I've been learning that while I can't determine in life when I'm going to get kicked, I can determine which way I'm going to go when it happens.

I can't determine in life when I'm going to get kicked, I can determine which way I'm going to go when it happens.

I guess there's no way to grow up without some going down. No humility without humiliations. A person becomes terribly frustrated and bitter if he ignores the law of *Flexible Planning.*

I heard about a boy who went to work in a grocery store after graduating from high school. A few weeks later his dad said, "Son, let's talk about college."

"Oh, Dad, I didn't tell you. I'm not going to college."

"You're not going to college? Why not?"

"I'm not going to college because I found my life's work."

"What do you mean you found your life's work?"

"You know," he said, "I love driving the truck to deliver groceries. The boss is happy; I just got a raise. It's really wonderful work."

"Well, son, you need to do something besides drive a truck and deliver groceries all your life."

The boy said, "Wait a minute. Didn't you tell me the point of life is to be happy?"

"Yes."

"Well, I'm happy now. I'm not going to college!"

His dad was the victim of his own myopia. The point of life isn't happiness. It's *growth.* The dad realized he had to take another approach. There was no use telling a sixteen-year-old the answers because sixteen-year-olds already have all the answers. So Dad went down to the grocery and said, "John, you're going to have to fire my son."

The point of life isn't happiness. It's *growth*.

"What do you mean, fire your son? I've never known a boy like this. He's the most wonderful boy I've ever seen. I just gave him a raise. Shines that truck. Keeps people happy. He's great!"

"Well, he doesn't want to go to college," said the father, "and if you don't fire him, you're going to ruin his life."

The grocer realized he had to do something. On Friday the kid came in to get his pay, and the grocer said, "Just a minute."

The kid said, "Yes?"

"You're fired."

"What'd I do?"

"You're fired."

"What's wrong?"

"You're fired!"

"Wh—"

"You're fired!"

The kid got the message. He went home, dejected. He said, "All right, Dad. I'll go to school."

Capitalize on your heartbreaks and misery or you'll miss the best in life.

This is a true story. Some thirty years later, after the boy had gone on to become president of one of the leading universities, he said to his dad, "I want to thank you for the time you got me fired."

It's a hard lesson to learn, but the law of *Flexible Planning* says to capitalize on your heartbreaks and misery or you'll miss the best in life. Make the things that go wrong a part of your plan, and you will be far ahead of where you were when you were waiting for something good to happen.

This doesn't mean you shouldn't plan. In 1918, Charles Schwab, president of Bethlehem Steel, granted an interview to Ivy Lee, an extraordinary management consultant. Lee told Schwab that his consulting firm could uncover opportunities for improvement in the company's operations. Schwab said he already knew of more things that should be done than he and his staff could handle. What was needed was "not more knowing, but more going."

What was needed was "not more knowing, but more going."

"If you can show us a way to get more things done," Schwab said, "I'll be glad to listen to you, and, if it works, I'll pay you whatever you ask within reason."

Lee answered, "If that is what you want, I will show you a method that will increase your personal management efficiency, and that of anyone else who applies it, by at least fifty percent."

He handed Schwab a blank piece of paper and said, "Write down the most important things you have to do tomorrow." Schwab did as requested. It took about five minutes.

Then Lee said, "Now number them in the order of their true importance." This took a little longer because Schwab wanted to be sure of what he was doing.

Finally, Lee instructed, "The first thing tomorrow morning, start working on item number one, and stay with it until it is completed. Then, take item number two the same way. Then, number three, and so on. Don't worry if you don't complete everything according to the schedule. At least you will have completed the most important projects before getting to the less important ones. If you can't finish all that you planned for tomorrow with this system, there's no other way you would have finished. And without this system you probably would have taken much longer to complete what you set out to do, without taking care of things in the order of their real value to you and your company.

"Do this every working day," Lee went on. "After you have convinced yourself of the value of this system, have your men try it. Try it as long as you like, and then send me your check for whatever you think the idea is worth."

In a few weeks, Charles Schwab sent Ivy Lee a check for $25,000. That was a lot of money in 1918.

Schwab reportedly stated that this lesson was the most profitable one he learned in his business career. It was later said that this was the plan largely responsible for turning a little steel company into one of the largest steel producers in the world. It also helped make Charles Schwab a multi-millionaire.

That's an incredibly simple way to plan your day to get the most out of the available time though it is not a strategy for accomplishing a goal. You need *Flexible Planning* for that.

Learn to capitalize on things that go wrong, making them stepping stones of progress.

Flexible Planning says you need a plan that enables you to roll with the punches, to adapt and adjust. Learn to capitalize on things that go wrong, making them stepping stones of progress. *Flexible Planning* will also make the *wrong* things *right*, an exchange that anyone should appreciate.

THE SIXTH FUNCTION OF FOLLOWERSHIP:

Flexible Planning

By: Tracey C. Jones

Are you willing to suffer for success? Mario Andretti once said, "If everything seems under control, you're not driving fast enough." The follower's path to leadership entails a great deal of blind turns, dead ends, and rerouting.

The reason I manage to maintain a happy disposition most of the time is because I expect everything to go wrong. And since it rarely does, I'm always delighted. Followers who stop in their tracks whenever something doesn't go as planned have a tough road. I may never achieve stratospheric levels of success, but one thing I do know how to do is respond when life throws me a curve ball. Whenever I get beat up, I know it's a chance for me to get upbeat because something good is going to happen as a result of the challenge.

The magic only happens outside of your comfort zone, so you're going to have to get comfortable taking leaps of faith and developing your wings on the way down. Really effective followers know how to build a fortress out of the bricks life throws at them. In fact, whenever someone would call my father and ask him to pray for their troubles, he would exclaim, "Why should I pray you out of something that God has put you in to make you stronger?" To this day I am certain he was the only man on the planet who routinely got notes from people pleading, "Please, Charlie, stop praying for me. I've had all I can take!"

The magic only happens outside of your comfort zone, so you're going to have to get comfortable taking leaps of faith and developing your wings on the way down.

Locus Focus is a term I concocted in my own cauldron of creativity to signify the extent to which individuals believe they can control events. Those with an external locus focus believe that outside forces, like luck, determine what happens to them. While people who develop an internal locus focus believe that they alone are responsible for their own successes and failures. It's a simple but incredibly powerful distinction that serves every individual well and deserves careful reflection. Followers who have mastered the Sixth Function know that their own internal locus of control determines the strength and latitude of their flexibility.

Do you believe life just happens to you? That it's written in the stars? That luck plays a big part? If something doesn't go your way, do you blame outside sources? Or, do you believe that you affect your life, that fate has nothing to do with it, and it's all about taking responsibility for your own actions?

At the core of this juxtaposition is the issue of control and how much power we think we have to influence outcomes. While no one can control every aspect of their existence (things like genetics, timing, family members, political and global landscapes, and the like), knowing what you *can* control is as important as knowing what you can't. Awareness, action, and attitude are all flexibility enhancers.

Awareness, action, and attitude are all flexibility enhancers.

Followers don't get fearful when the rug is yanked out from under them. Remember, if you want to be a diamond, you're going to have to get cut. Flexible planning is the key to falling forward. We keep our eye on the end goal, but the strategies and routes that get us there are completely fluid and mutable.

We are like glow-sticks; only when we're broken do we get the chance to shine. We can take the flaws and turn them into something flawsome!

Whatever can go wrong will go wrong. But your determination is what will cause you to persevere or lay down and die. One of the key tenets of flexible followership is the desire to stay relevant. Ask yourself: How can I be of greater service and use to my leaders? This will drive you to invest in your own personal research and development. I worked in a lot of scientific and technology groups in my career. Research and development always drove production and sales. We need to do the same thing for ourselves. If the company won't or can't provide training, *you* shell out the money. You are the only one who can manage your career. Take control of it. Invest in you.

You are the only one who can manage your career. Take control of it. Invest in you.

In *The Power of Followership*, Robert Kelley says, "The responsibility for maintaining leading-edge skills is yours, not the organization's. If you depend on the organization or the leader for maintaining those skills, you will be sadly disappointed." By investing in yourself, you'll be ready to weather and adapt to any reduction in force, buyout, merger, acquisition, downsizing, or opportunity that comes your way. I am amazed when people are crushed because their job of 'x' number of years is no longer an option. Why did they think that life came with guarantees?

The best thing you can do as a follower is to constantly improve your skills. Find out if your employer will cover any of your schooling. Guess what I did when the tech sector took a downturn in the early 2000's? I got my MBA, and my employer reimbursed a large portion of it. My father used to say, "Life isn't mainly a matter of doing what you like to do; it's doing what you ought to do and need to do."

Another thing that always shocks me is when followers lament that they can't find a job that allows them to do what *they* want to do. Who said anything about getting to do what *you* want to do? If you have an opportunity to do anything, take it. In the process, you will acquire experiences and discipline and character. When life finally decides you're ready to begin excelling at what it put you on Earth to do, you can do it in a tremendous way.

Don't have a job you love or a leader you respect? Don't worry about it. Nothing is forever, and you'll have numerous opportunities to develop your followership flexibility in the years to come. This is why the function of flexible planning is so critical to your success. Get clear on your identity, focus on the goal, and adjust the required steps.

Get clear on your identity, focus on the goal, and adjust the required steps.

In order to get clear on your identity I recommend you take as many personal assessments as you can. These range from DISC® and Myers-Briggs® to StrengthsFinder® and StandOut 2.0 assessments. You can also take Robert Kelley's followership personality profile for free online. These tools will help you discover the best working environments for your particular skills. They can save you time and frustration by helping you make the next right step.

Flexible followers don't panic when the leader makes a change. They understand that the only unchanging thing in the world is *change.* They understand that change is a byproduct of external factors as well as the need for the organization to constantly be creative and reinvent itself. They thrive on change because they have honed their flexibility chops. They know they'll always find a way, and, even if the organization closes, they'll always land on their feet.

Look, leaders rarely hand new challenges to followers whom they know can't handle change. They don't go to the ones who ask, "Why is this happening?" They go to the ones who ask, "How can we make this happen?"

Flexible followership gives you the freedom to create your own best leadership path. Don't just seek to become *rich;* seek rather to *enrich.*

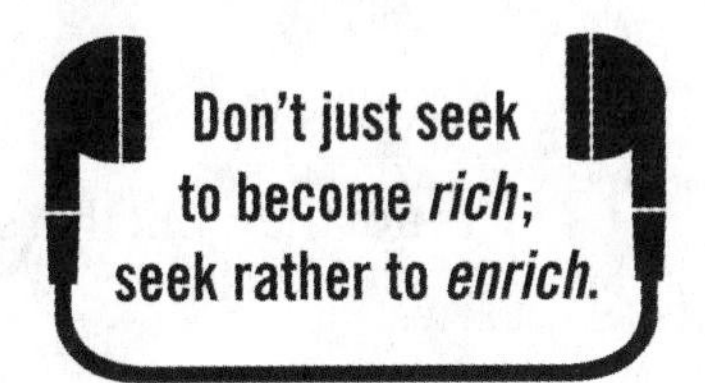

They say there are three answers to the questions we ask God: "yes," "no," and "I've got something better for you." Flexible planning allows us to know that, whatever His response, there's a reason for it. And that reason is to make us more determined followers in the short term and better leaders in the long run. Whatever happens, it's up to each of us to determine the appropriate responses and best relationships that will garner the most tremendous outcomes.

—POINTS TO PONDER—

- What good can come out of the bad that just happened?
- Look at the person who got the position and try to spot areas for development.
- Nothing works, gets used to it.
- It's not the event that's important it's your response to it.

MILLENNIAL MOMENT #7:
Have you ever said this?

My boss is an idiot!

I know with certainty and experience that there are employers out there who, on a very real, very personal level, stink. But so what?

Despite all these surveys—the snapshot and more detailed varieties—putting it squarely on the shoulders of the employer to "fix" things is something you simply cannot control. You know what you can control? YOU. You control your attitude, your work ethic, your willingness to step up and do the needful. You control how you treat your coworkers, your customers, and yes, your boss.

Yes, your bosses should do a better job. But that's on them, not on you.

Someday, when you finally get to sit at the helm, you're going to realize that there's a heckuva lot more going on than you imagined. Until you formally wear the title, you have no idea what it actually means to be responsible for, well, everything. So until that day comes, try to give your boss the benefit of the doubt. You're not going to understand every decision—and you certainly won't like every task. But you have a responsibility *to yourself* to do the best you can—and that responsibility is not negated by your dislike of the person in charge.

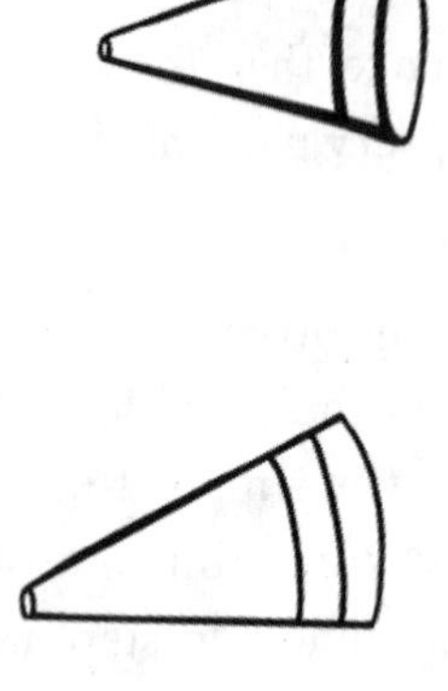

You are your own best advocate. Don't rely on the approval and praise of others to recognize the greatness in yourself. Self-awareness and self-respect are two of the greatest traits of followership and leadership.

THE SEVENTH LAW OF LEADERSHIP:

Motivated to Motivating

By: Charlie "Tremendous" Jones

Today we're surrounded by motivators. People and things strive to motivate us to buy a product, pay for advice, or enlist in a cause. Motivation classes are crammed, and motivational books are bestsellers. Motivation is big business!

But look closely at these motivators. Some reach the point where they can motivate anybody into doing anything, and success is running out their ears, yet they are miserable because they forgot to learn how to motivate themselves! The motivator who can motivate everybody but himself may win the world, but he'll never enjoy it.

Which would you rather be—a miserable, successful motivator or a happy, motivated flop? I would rather be a happy, motivated flop. If I am learning to be motivated, I'll eventually become a successful motivator of others, and I'll be happy doing it. How well I remember my great desire as a young salesman to become a master motivator. I couldn't wait to finish my training so I could use my dynamic motivational skills. My sales presentations were powerful. In fact, they were so powerful that I felt I had to temper them or the prospect might die of a heart attack before I asked him to buy. I knew no one could resist the logic, the benefits, the security, the peace of mind—there hardly seemed a problem in the world that my presentation couldn't solve!

My heart would hit the floor. I'd sink so low I'd have to reach up to touch bottom.

I recall how I expected the prospect to snatch the pen from my hand and sign on the dotted line—but the prospect never did. Right in the hottest part of the sizzle, my prospect would yawn or interrupt with some scintillating statement like, "I'm insurance-poor," or "I have $5,000 with double *identity!*"

My heart would hit the floor. I'd sink so low I'd have to reach up to touch bottom. You never saw a more discouraged young salesman than I was. I soon learned that my problem wasn't how to motivate. My problem was keeping the customer from demotivating me!

Sometimes I became so discouraged there was nothing to do but cry on the boss's shoulder, only to find out he was more discouraged than me. The prospects were discouraging me, the boss was discouraging me, friends were discouraging me, and I thought at times even my wife was discouraging me.

Sometimes a fellow at a seminar will come up and murmur, "Do you know why I'm not a success? I have a miserable wife."

I enjoy giving these fellows the shock treatment: "Do you really have a miserable wife? Well, you don't know how lucky you are. The best asset a man can have is a *miserable wife!* What if my wife had been sympathetic when I went home and told her how miserable things were and she said, 'Oh, my sweet little hubby, you stay home here with me, and I'll take care of you'? We would have consoled each other amongst our furniture on the sidewalk!"

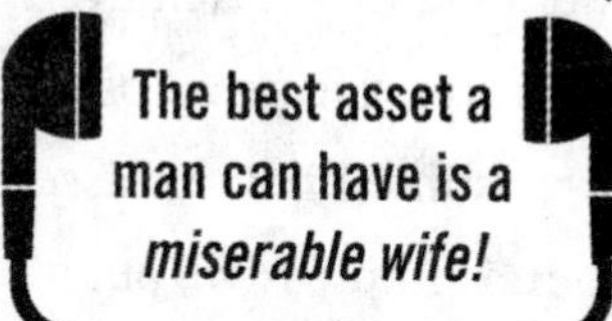

If you have a miserable wife, you'll keep working, or she'll remind you what an idiot you were to take such a job in the first place. But don't despair if you don't have a miserable wife. You can probably make the grade without this asset.

I'm kidding, but I want to make it clear that there are no barriers you can't overcome when you learn to be motivated. I believe with all my heart that everything that touches your life can make you a more deeply motivated person who in turn can motivate others to higher goals.

There are no barriers you can't overcome when you learn to be motivated.

Some people ask me for my secret to staying motivated. Well, I never found it. It found me. One of my achievements during my first five years in sales was five years of consecutive weekly production. This means that I never missed one week of selling a policy. This sounds impressive, but it's not the whole truth.

The whole truth is that I believed in goals, and so I made a vow that I would sell a policy every week *or buy one.* After I bought twenty-two policies, I began to get motivated. I didn't realize that a simple vow would have the power to influence my work for the rest of my life. That vow, and what it cost me to keep it, began to teach me *involvement and commitment.*

Some people get involved with their work but lack commitment. Others are committed but don't get deeply involved. The two go together, and I'm convinced that there is no way to learn to be a motivated person in whatever venture you are engaged unless you are both totally involved and committed.

The greatest motivations I've had come from my own heart and home. Someone else's experience or story will never motivate you as deeply as your own.

I used to tell a prospect who said he was insurance-poor that he was actually insurance-rich. But I discovered something far more effective through a little episode at home. This experience allowed me to agree wholeheartedly with an insurance-poor prospect but it gave me additional motivation to pass on to him. This is what happened.

"I can't wait to be successful so I can move to a plush office downtown where I can fail in style."

My son Jere, who was six-years-old at the time, came in from the yard one day yelling at the top of his lungs for his mother. Naturally, this distracted me from my work in my office (actually, it was our living room. We had moved the furniture into the hallway). Jere upped his yell several decibels, and I thought, "I can't wait to be successful so I can move to a plush office downtown where I can fail in style."

Finally, Jere gave up, and just then Gloria came up from the basement where she had been running the washer. She said, "What did you want, Jere?" He replied, "Nothing. I just wanted to know where you were."

I've told that story thousands of times because it shows why I pay the premiums on those twenty-two policies. I may never leave my six children an empire, a block of real estate, or a huge stock portfolio, but I'm going to leave them a priceless gift: a full-time mother. Because of my life insurance all six could come yelling for their mother, any time of the day, knowing she was somewhere around the house even though she didn't answer.

Another time I was sitting in the rocker reading the paper when eight-year-old Pam slipped her little blonde head under my arm and wiggled onto my lap. I kept reading, but then she said those few words that have helped me sell millions of dollars in life insurance. Looking at me with big, sad eyes, she said, "Daddy, if you won't ever leave me, I won't ever leave you."

I couldn't understand what prompted those words, but I immediately thought, "Well, dearest, I would never leave you, but if the Lord should rule otherwise, at least I'll never leave you *without.*"

Years ago I learned there were two kinds of dads, the see-kind and the have-kind. The see-kind says, "I want my family to have everything I can give them as long as I'm here to see it." The have-kind says, "I want them to have it whether I'm here to see it or not."

These simple family episodes shaped my views on commitment and involvement.

You say, "I'm not in the insurance field," or "I don't have a selling career." The principles we are talking about are the same for a student, a spouse, an office worker, a salesperson, or whatever you are. The great things in your life will be greater if you capitalize on them to help you *be motivated.* Remember, you are building a life, not an empire.

Everything in your life works together to help you become a more deeply motivated person.

I've heard people say, "I put my business first," and others say, "I put my family first." A few say, "I put my church first." (The truth is they probably put themselves first.) But I've found that my best lessons for business come from my family and my church. And the best lessons for my family come from my business and church. And the best lessons for church come from my family and my business. Everything in your life works together to help you become a more deeply motivated person.

One of the best stories I've heard that shows the difference between outward and inward motivation is told by Bob Richards, the former pole-vault champion. A college boy on the football team was a number-one goof-off, a goldbricker. He liked to hear the cheers, but he didn't like to charge the line. He liked to wear the suit, but he didn't like to practice. Basically, he didn't like to work.

One day the players were doing fifty laps, and this showpiece was doing his usual five. The coach came over and said, "Hey, kid, here's a telegram for you."

The kid said, "Read it for me, coach." He was so lazy he didn't even like to read.

Coach opened it up and read, "Dear son, your father's dead. Come home immediately." The coach swallowed hard. He said, "Take the rest of the week off." He didn't care if he took the rest of the *year* off.

When game time came on Friday, and the team rushed out on the field, lo and behold, the last kid out was the goof-off. No sooner did the gun sound than the kid was saying, "Coach, can I play today? Can I play?"

The coach thought, "Kid, you're not playing today. This is homecoming. This is the big game. We need every real guy we have, and you're not one of them."

Every time the coach turned around, the kid badgered him. "Coach, please let me play. Coach, I've got to play."

The first quarter ended with the score lopsided against the old alma mater. At halftime the coach braced them in the locker room with a fight talk. "All right, men, get out there and hit 'em. This is a long way from being over. Win this one for the old coacheroo!"

The team rushed out and began stumbling around again. The coach mumbled to himself and started to write his resignation. And up came this kid again. "Coach, coach, let me play, please!" The coach looked up at the scoreboard. "All right," he said, "get in there, kid. You can't hurt nothin' now."

No sooner did the kid hit the field than his team began to explode. He ran, passed, blocked, and tackled like a star. The electricity leaped to the team. The score began to even up. In the closing seconds of the game this kid intercepted a pass and ran all the way for the winning touchdown.

The stands broke loose. Pandemonium. People hoisted the hero onto their shoulders. Such cheering you never heard. Finally, the excitement subsided, and the coach got over to the kid and said, "I never saw anything like that. What in the world happened to you out there?"

He said, "Coach, you know my dad died last week."

"Yes," he said, "I read you the telegram."

"Well, coach, my dad was blind. And today was the first day he ever saw me play!"

Wouldn't it be great if life were a game? Wouldn't it be wonderful if the field of life had cheering sections on each side? Then, when we reached the impossible situation and didn't know how to go on, and no one understood us and we're about ready to fold and say those terrible words, "I quit," wouldn't it be wonderful if the fans would come alive and yell, "Charlie, boy, keep on going. We're with you!" I'd say, "That's all I needed." Boy, I'd run on down the field for another touchdown.

Those who know how to be motivated don't need a cheering section. They have built-in motivation.

But life isn't a game, is it? It's a battlefield. Instead of players and spectators, we're all soldiers, including some goldbrickers and some AWOLs. But we're all in the struggle, whether we know it or not. Those who know how to be motivated don't need a cheering section. They have built-in motivation. They don't look for a crutch that might break or a bonus that will be taxed away. They learn motivation from within. What really *makes* you is your inner dynamic and the learning of the law of being motivated, not the power of motivating others. If you are motivated, you will motivate others inevitably. And isn't it exciting to be around people who are motivated?

If you are motivated, you will motivate others inevitably.

I hope this helps you frame your thoughts with words so you can think through these laws you've already known instinctively. Our innate notions about these laws are basically correct, but so many things in life seem at war against them in an attempt to disprove them. Practice will prove them, and only the people who are exercising these basic laws will move ahead and grow in leadership. Do yourself a favor. Learn this law of leadership.

THE SEVENTH FUNCTION OF FOLLOWERSHIP:

Motivated to Motivating

By: Tracey C. Jones

Times were tough. A young man, desperate and broke, went to the zoo to look for a job. The zoo keeper told him that times were tough there, too. The gorilla recently died, and they didn't have enough money to buy another one. He told the young man to put on a gorilla costume and jump around the cage in an effort to keep customers coming. Hungry for work, he immediately said yes, put on the costume, and started jumping around and swinging from the branches. After a while, he noticed that the higher he would jump and swing the larger the crowd he drew and the louder their applause.

One day he got to swinging so high that the rope broke, and he flew out of the gorilla cage and landed right smack in the middle of the lion's den. He saw the lions charging toward him, and he yelled at the top of his lungs, "HELP, HELP! SOMEBODY SAVE ME!"

One of the lions caught him, spun him around, grabbed him by the neck, and snarled, "You better shut up, or we're all gonna get fired!!"

As Bum Philips said, "The only form of discipline that lasts is self-discipline."

Did you know that exemplary followers learn to develop their own inner cheering section? They don't rely on rewards, sticks, carrots, or threats to get them moving in the right direction. Their own sense of self-efficacy is so highly developed that they don't just do the best thing; they do the *right* thing in the interest of the organization. Rodney Dangerfield said, "Men who do things without having to be told draw the most wages." We're all adults. We shouldn't have to wait for our leaders to come and tell us to do the things we know we ought to do.

Booker T. Washington explained motivated followership in crystal clear terms: "You want to get to the point where you can anticipate the wants of your employer. In this way you will make yourself of greater service to him." Noble leaders value exemplary followers who act of their own accord. Be a follower who takes care of every single problem or situation that comes to your attention. Don't be the one who says, "That's not my job," or "Let's wait until someone tells us to do it."

The Law of Inertia applies not only to physical objects but also to human attitudes. A body at rest tends to stay at rest unless acted upon by an outside force. That force is the exemplary follower. Every follower has a decision to make: Are you going to be a thermostat or a thermometer? Are you going to go into the organization and be passive, merely reflecting what's going on around you, or are you going to take an active stance and go into your work space to create atmosphere? My father always told me, "Anybody knows that atmosphere doesn't come out of thin air. Somebody has to create it." And if you can't create it as a Function of Followership, you will never be able to sustain it while living the Laws of Leadership. Today is a great day to learn how to get excited about your work. Do it now and watch your future unfold.

Today is a great day to learn how to get excited about your work.

Speaking of laws of physics, here's another formula for exemplary followers to apply: F= ma, force equals mass times acceleration. If you want a greater force in your life, if you want to make a more pronounced impact, if you want to get yourself off your "mass," you've got to apply an accelerant.

That accelerant is motivation. It is the only thing that will keep your rockets ignited when dealing with the highs and lows on the pathway to leadership. William Penn put it best: "No man is fit to command another that cannot command himself." If you can't motivate yourself, don't expect your boss, your spouse, your church, your finances, or anything else to be able to light your fires. If you aren't fired with motivation, chances are you'll just be *fired.*

The beauty of motivation is that it has a synergistic effect. The more motivated you are as a follower, the more motivated your teammates tend to be. And trust me, leaders notice which groups are thriving and which ones are just surviving in terms of energy and work ethic.

Robert Kelley makes a great point for exemplary followers: "If you are going to drink from the organizational well, you must also help replenish it." Again, tremendous followers don't just do what needs to be done because of what's in it for them. They remain committed to making the entire entity a more motivated place. Your ability to do this will make you invaluable to the organization.

Before you can make that transition from exemplary follower to leader, you'll need to learn the art of self-management. Truly, the most important part of management is managing yourself. This includes staying focused on people and books that will hone your sense of personal motivation. You need to do this every day for the rest of your life.

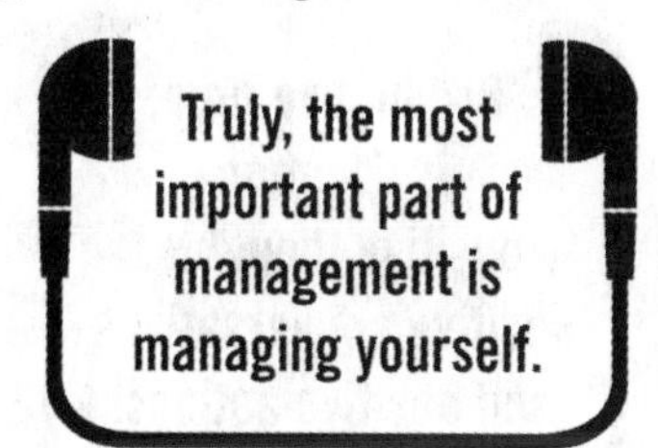

As long as you are breathing, you need to be reading. Life has a way of wearing us down every single moment. It's the Second Law of Thermodynamics: Everything tends toward a state of disarray and disorder, including you.

It takes a tremendous amount of work to stay motivated. My father used to say that your real task isn't keeping yourself motivated; it's keeping others from demotivating *you!* Zig Ziglar said it best: "They say motivation doesn't last. Well, neither does bathing. That's why we recommend it daily."

Wise followers know that leadership takes time. It requires seasoning. For us, it's not a matter of "if" but of "when," and that sometimes takes a lifetime. That's why we need to stay *motivated to motivating* so we don't quit right on the verge of our biggest breakthrough.

Napoleon Hill said, "Effort only fully releases its reward after a person refuses to quit." We need to fill time not kill time. Sitting at your job, doing the bare minimum, is a waste on so many levels. Productive time is spent on positive thoughts, positive conversations and positive actions. They say you can't change the people around you, but you can change the people you choose to be around. Remember, people are either a fountain or a drain. Be the fountain. Pour your life into others, and steer clear of the drains. Make sure to surround yourself with exemplary followers and learn from them. Be among other motivated individuals who compliment your energy and inspire you to climb to levels higher than you ever could have achieved on your own.

Productive time is spent on positive thoughts, positive conversations and positive actions.

—POINTS TO PONDER—

- The jerk store called. They're not running out of anyone. How can you keep them from demotivating you?
- What truly motivates me?
- What do I need to change about myself?
- Am I willing to make the investment in myself to get to where I need to be?

CONCLUSION

Throughout this book, there is a definitive relationship between Leadership and Followership. They are two sides to the same coin and reflect the duality found in everything: right brain vs left brain; emotive vs thinking; law vs mercy; individualistic vs collective; good vs evil; light vs dark. As you can see in the Leadership Followership Synergy graphic, on page 153, you need to have both qualities to end up where you ought to be.

The cost of non-followership is profound. You will be incarcerated by society if you refuse to follow the law. You will be terminated by your employer if you don't follow the rules. You will be distanced from your loved ones if you don't honor your vows. Duplicity and sincerity are at stark odds with each other. Choose the former and it will cost you and everyone around you. Choose the latter, and achieve everything in life you've ever wanted.

While it's important to understand where your strengths are and there are a number of incredible tests you can take, you also need to understand what type of follower you are. This allows you to pinpoint what type of leadership you work best under. Are you a maverick? Better work for a boss that allows you the latitude to co-lead. Do you want the boss to tell you exactly what to do? Better find a supervisor who doesn't expect you to come up with your own way of doing things.

Take the free followership test at http://www.gfwcflorida.org/juniors/progsjrs/Handout%20A.pdf. It's based on Robert Kelley's book, *The Power of Followership*. Had I taken it at your age, it might have saved me, and probably many of my bosses, a great deal of heartache.

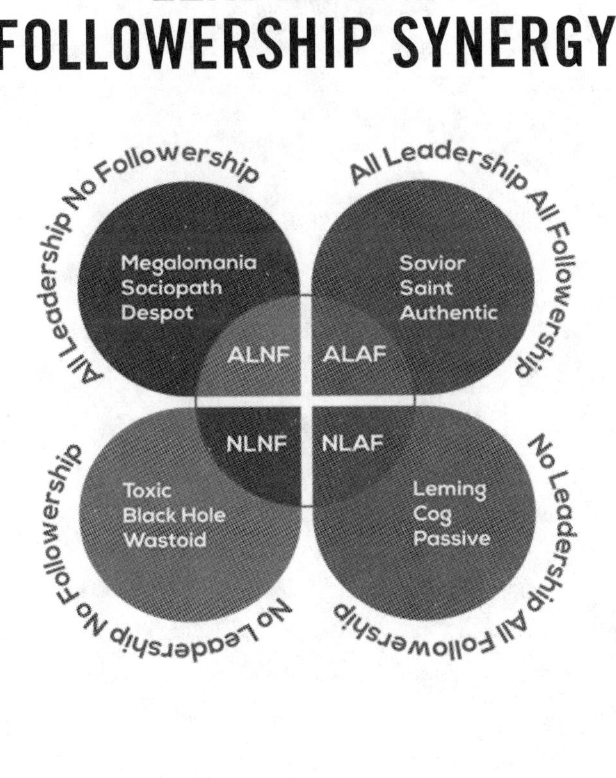
LEADERSHIP
FOLLOWERSHIP SYNERGY
All Leadership No Followership
All Leadership All Followership
No Leadership No Followership
No Leadership All Followership
Megalomania
Sociopath
Despot
Savior
Saint
Authentic
ALNF
ALAF
NLNF
NLAF
Toxic
Black Hole
Wastoid
Leming
Cog
Passive

ABC's FOR MILLENNIALS

"If you want this, you've got to do that."

With this adage in mind, here is a simple guideline that illustrates what must be done in order to achieve your desired results. The list is meant to be humorous, but it's also the truth. We often want the payoff without the hard work. That's the classic definition of greed, and no employer, friend, or partner aspires to greed. Find out what you want and then work for it.

Here are some truths to help you reach your goals.

Actions before Accolades

Buildup before Breakthrough

Commitment before Consummation

Discipline before Designation

Effort before Earning

Followership before Fanfare

Grunge before Glamour

Humility before Honor

Initiative before Influence

Justice before Justification

Knowledge before Know-it-all

Learning before Leading

Motivation before Mobility

Noticed before Nomination

Obedience before Obtaining

Productivity before Promotion

Quality before Quiddity

Results before Recognition

Sacrifices before Success

Teachability before Tenure

Understanding before Unity

Vision before Vow

Work before Win

X-ray vision before Xyzzy

Yearn before Yield

Zeal before Zenith

RECOMMENDED READING FOR MOTIVATED FOLLOWERS

Carnegie, Andrew.
The Advantages of Poverty

Collins, Jim.
Good to Great

Drummond, Henry.
The Greatest Thing in the World

Gray, Albert E. N.
The New Common Denominator of Success

Frankl, Victor E.
Man's Search for Meaning

Hubbard, Elbert.
A Message to Garcia

Jones, Charlie "Tremendous".
Mystery of Self-Motivation

Jones, Charlie "Tremendous".
Key to Excellence

Kelley, Robert.
The Power of Followership

Patton, General George S.
The Wit and Wisdom of General George S. Patton

Washington, Booker T.
Character Building

ABOUT THE AUTHOR

Charlie "Tremendous" Jones

Recently named one of the top 25 Legends of Personal Development, Charlie "Tremendous" Jones legacy spanned more than half a century and his book, *Life is Tremendous*, has sold millions of copies. Over 6000 audiences throughout the world have laughed while listening to Charlie Jones share his ideas about life's most challenging situations in business and at home. Known by his "Tremendous" nickname and humor, he is a recipient of the CPAE designation and the prestigious Cavett Award from the National Speakers Association.

Charlie Jones entered the insurance business at age 22 with one of America's top ten companies. At age 23, he was awarded his agency's most valuable associate award. Ten years later, he received his company's management award for recruiting and business management.

At age 37, his organization exceeded $100 million in sales, at which time he founded Life Management Services, Inc. to share his experience through seminars and consulting services. After his passing in October 2008, his daughter Tracey returned to pick up the mantel of leadership and continue the "Tremendous" legacy. Charlie is best remembered for his mantra, "You'll be the same person five years from now that you are today except for two things; the people you meet and the books you read." His legacy continues to be shared around the world and is impacting the next generation of leaders.

ABOUT THE AUTHOR

Tracey C. Jones

Tracey took her father's advice to heart and has led a diverse career. She graduated from New Mexico Military Institute, the United States Air Force Academy and then spent 12 years living all over the world fixing fighter jets. After her time in the military, she stepped into the high volume manufacturing world of semi-conductors where she honed her project management skills. There she learned the pain of being responsible for everything, but in control of nothing. Tracey's next move was to increased roles in defense contracting positions where she continued to hone her people skills and operational expertise.

She is currently working on her doctorate in Leadership and learning something new each day. Tracey's passion includes helping others realize their potential and to discover ways they can begin making a difference in their own life immediately.

For other leadership titles
be sure to visit

www.Tremendousleadership.com

For bulk and international orders
contact us directly at:

717-701-8159

or email:

info@tremendousleadership.com

Other leadership titles from

Tracey C. Jones

TREMENDOUS TRACEY

Leadership with a kick

Book Tracey as a speaker
for your next event!

www.tremendoustracey.com

P.O. Box 267
Boiling Springs, PA 17007

Phone: 717-701-8159
info@tremendousleadership.com

Tremendous Notes

Tremendous Notes

Tremendous Notes

Tremendous Notes

Tremendous Notes

Tremendous Notes

Tremendous Notes

Tremendous Notes

Tremendous Notes